PRAISE FOR BREAKING GENERATIONAL CHAINS AND DR. PATRICIA BARRINGTON:

"Powerful, Complete and Comprehensive!"
–Jan Payne, Success Coach with the Brian Tracy Organization

"The book is wonderful. I preached a message from it last Sunday about generational chains and both brothers and sisters opened their spiritual eyes to the struggles and disorders they face. I am so appreciative for this revelation about the generational chains. The book has an anointed massage, which people need to hear. People are tired of hearing they are blessed, but still finding themselves facing the same problems. This book shows how to break the chains at the root of the problems, so life can truly change. Thank you, Dr. Barrington. May God bless you."
–Pastor Grace Omundi

I thank God for this work. It is a real masterpiece—holistic and generally tailored for the present-day church, which needs a divine intervention in this area! I encourage all saints to read this book and discover life as God meant you to live it.
—Rev. Robert Nyamwange, Kissi, Kenya

"Breaking Generational Chains left me with a sense of deliverance and freedom. I am confident in preaching its truths to my members and helping them find greater freedom in Christ. This book is fodder enough for liberation.

Dr. Patricia has great experience and exposure. In Kenya alone, she founded three missions, Nairobi, Nakuru and Kisii —each has its own school, orphanage and church. She is an amazing example of a Proverbs 31 woman using what God has given her. She has overcome great odds to cross borders and reached the vulnerable.

In Kenya East Africa, she is known to be a transformative educator in biblical knowledge; she is an eloquent minister of the gospel and has helped restore many lives through her charity work and empowerment.

This book is a great resource for both believer and nonbeliever to help them move beyond mediocrity, struggles and defeat, which result from generational issues.

God bless you Dr. Patricia for allowing God to use you as a vessel for His glorious work."

—Pastor Peter Moturi, Bread and Soup Ministry Nakuru Solai, KENYA EAST AFRICA

Breaking

GENERATIONAL

Chains

A Woman's Guide to Freedom

DR. PATRICIA BARRINGTON, M.ED., TH.D.

Lionfish

Breaking Generational Chains—A Woman's Guide to Freedom
by Dr. Patricia Barrington, M.ED., TH.D.
Copyright ©2016 Dr. Patricia Barrington

Published by Lionfish Books, an imprint of Media City Publishers,
Los Angeles, CA
Cover design and layout by: Jana Rade, Impact studios
Lionfish   Edited by: Maria Lewytzkyj-Milligan

Author's Website and Blog: www.DrPatriciaBarrington.com
Follow Dr. Barrington on Twitter: Twitter.com/PBarrington57
Facebook Book Page at: Facebook.com/pbfreeme
Instagram: pbfreeme
LinkedIn/Email: breadandsoup@gmail.com

FIRST EDITION: September 2016

Library of Congress Control Number: 2016954189

Barrington, Patricia
Breaking Generational Chains : A woman's guide to freedom

Paperback ISBN: 9780981898384

Foreword

It is a proven fact that the lives and fortunes of persons are affected by the activities of their forbears. This is not only true physically, but also psycho-logically and most importantly, spiritually. The question that remains is whether these affects are caused by God, by renegade demons or by us.

In Ezekiel 18:1-3, God forbade the use of the proverb, which states, "The parents ate the sour grapes, but the children got the sour taste." From that day forward, God declared that each generation was responsible for its sin. In Colossians 2:11-15, it is reported that God has erased the law that condemned us by nailing it to Christ's cross, thus disarming Satan and his minions. Although God is not enforcing generational curses, we remain in chains because of our sin and doubt.

In this book, Dr. Patricia Barrington explores the root causes of some of the difficulties many experience and the road to victory over them. May we think and learn to walk through the grace of God in our Lord Jesus.

Christ has redeemed us from the curse of the law having become a curse for us … that the blessing of Abraham might come upon the Gentiles in Christ Jesus …

Dr. Victor O Taylor

Dedication

Dedicated to my daughter, Lauren Moriah who helped me to break the mother daughter generational chains in my family. And to my son, Rudolph Montgomery.

Acknowledgements

To write a book like this takes perseverance, pushing through a lot of pain and fighting battles of spiritual warfare. However, I want to thank all the amazing people who surrounded my life during this process and prayed for and with me.

Thank you to Sister Deborah Norman for all of your support, encouragement and for entering with me into spiritual warfare at the beginning of this process. Thank you to Margarita Melendez and Gordon Blaise, the paraprofessionals who constantly reminded me to write this book because the information could help someone. Thank you to my cousin Cornelia and my friend Leona who spend many hours with me on the phone talking about this topic. I would also like to thank the sisters who have accompanied me on my treks to the mission field: Elder Pamela Gibbs, Elder Francis Bell, Sister Deborah Norman, Little Sister Lauren Barrington, Prophetess Lisa Cooper and Evangelist Chardonea Wright.

Thank you to Mr. T.R. Locke, and everyone at Lionfish Books and Media City Publishing, for your vision and for working with me to put this book together and get it out.

Contents

Introduction

Whitney Houston was one of the greatest singers ever. God blessed her with a voice unlike anyone before her. No one could sing so powerfully and make it look as easy as she could. She was an amazing woman. At the height of her career in the '90s, her voice led her to international fame as the most successful female singer in history. She could afford anything her heart desired. Her life was one of riches, fame, power, and an endless supply of generous material benefits.

Whitney was both an international singing star and an international movie star. She has received Oscars, Grammys, and every award any organization ever thought to give out. She traveled in private planes, chauffeured cars and had more than most people even dream. She could have done anything with her life. She could have used her power, wealth and influence as a platform to change the world.

Sadly, Whitney had another side to her. Although people knew about her erratic behavior and had witnessed her struggle with drugs, few people knew the depth of her problem. Even fewer knew the root cause. Whitney had the world, but something else had Whitney. Whitney was chained to addiction. But what caused it? Why? Why would someone who had the world in her hands need to numb herself though drugs? What was going on inside Whitney Houston that led to her being found overdosed and dead in a Beverly Hills Hilton bathtub?

Certainly, there are lots of temptations for superstars. Whatever they want is available to them on a silver platter, and certainly there are people around them who would love for them to be intoxicated, dependent and disoriented. It's much easier to take advantage of such a person. Whitney's addiction may well have been a benefit to others as much as it was a detriment to Whitney.

However, a possible clue to the reason for her struggle can be found in a few obscure articles online. At one time in her career, Whitney Houston's father sued her for one hundred million dollars. As part of the justification for the lawsuit, her father argued that he helped get a case for marijuana possession wiped from Whitney's record. Her father allegedly pleaded with her from a national news show, "Get yourself together and give me the money you owe me."

Whether Mr. Houston believed that getting a marijuana case dismissed was worth one hundred million dollars or not, it seems pretty clear that a father willing to sue his daughter for one hundred million dollars has got some issues. Issues he likely passed down to that daughter. Issues, it now seems, Whitney passed down to her own daughter. Three years after Whitney's mysterious and tragic death, Bobbi Kristina Houston, Whitney's 22-year-old daughter, also died, intoxicated in a bathtub, just as her mother Whitney had died.

Interestingly, both Whitney and Bobbi Kristina were attracted to and involved with alleged drug addicts—Bobby Brown, Whitney's husband, and Nick Gordon, Bobbi's boyfriend. Why?

The answer this book will suggest is that long-standing violations of God's principles for living have contributed to a psychological, social, mental, emotional and spiritual phenomenon best described as generational chains or curses, which have profound negative effects on families and individuals for years beyond the life of the offending person. These chains have the power to destroy even the greatest personal achievements because they are spiritually-based issues that cannot be resolved with physical or material solutions.

My goal for my sisters who read this book is that they would be spared the chains that plagued Whitney Houston and her daughter. My goal is to ensure that my sisters have the power and knowledge to:

- Identify and combat the effects of generational chains
- Make sense of your life and life choices
- Value your identity and purpose in accordance with God's plan
- Follow a scriptural path to spiritual, emotional, and social healing
- Create a new pattern of generational blessings and wholeness
- Sustain a life of spiritual power and success

The effects of generational chains can be broken if the right Biblical principles are accessed and applied. You do not need to be victims of the sins of your fathers and mothers. The Bible affords answers to forge a new path in life, break generational chains, and replace them with generational blessings and favor.

My work as an educator, charity organizer and minister has taken me from the United States to the Caribbean to and to multiple countries in Africa, including Kenya, Ethiopia, Tanzania, Uganda and East Africa. I have seen first-hand the effect of generational chains and curses and I have worked in helping many break free from their bondage.

My prayer for you is that you will join me on this journey of self-discovery, empowerment and abundance, and that you will break free from any generational chains that cripple your life.

Chapter 1

KNOWING YOUR PURPOSE: LIFE AND CALLING

"For God has not given us a spirit of fear and timidity, but of power, love and self-discipline." ~2 Timothy 1:7

Who are you, and what is your purpose?

My sister, you and I are individuals, yet we are actually small parts of a larger body called "a community." In this community, we have unique roles to play. It is absolutely true that each of us, no matter how similar, is different from other members of the community. Each of us is born with gifts and talents that we must share with the community at large in order to benefit the physical, spiritual, mental, and emotional well-being of all.

In some ways, we share our talents and gifts with our local group—we are mothers, sisters, friends, cousins, and aunties. In other ways, we share our talents and gifts with those outside our immediate group as teachers, business leaders, doctors, chefs, nurses, pastors, police officers, or therapists. Although it does not always feel like it, even those who seem to be strangers are members of our community. And contrary to what Cain answered in reply to God's question, we are all our sister's guardians.

God's Word: Genesis 4:1-9: The Cain and Able Story:

Now Adam had sexual relations with his wife, Eve, and she became pregnant. When she gave birth to Cain, she said, "With the Lord's help, I have produced a man!" Later she gave birth to his brother and named him Abel.

When they grew up, Abel became a shepherd, while Cain cultivated the ground.

When it was time for the harvest, Cain presented some of his crops as a gift to the Lord. Abel also brought a gift—the best of the firstborn lambs from his flock. The Lord accepted Abel and his gift, but he did not accept Cain and his gift. This made Cain very angry, and he looked dejected.

"Why are you so angry?" the Lord asked Cain. "Why do you look so dejected? If you had done the right thing, you would be smiling; but because you have done evil, sin is crouching at your door. It wants to rule you, but you must overcome it." Then Cain suggested to his brother, "Let's go

out into the fields." And while they were in the field, Cain attacked his brother, Abel, and killed him.

Afterward the Lord asked Cain, "Where is your brother? Where is Abel?"

"I don't know," Cain responded. "Am I my brother's guardian?"

Consider the story here. Even if you agree with the idea that all humanity is related, certainly you recognize that we still do very cruel things to each other. Cain was Abel's actual brother. The two grew up together and played together. In fact, as the first two children of the first two humans, they had no choice. They were each other's only companions besides their parents. Yet, Cain, in a fit of jealousy over a sacrifice offered to God, killed his brother. Since that first murder—that first separation from God's social order—we all seem to have forgotten our common humanity and bonds.

As generational descendants of this troubled family, we view each other as competitors for limited resources—be those resources money, opportunities, approval, or even parental or social love. We divide into small groups against each other and praise our own group as if it could function independently of others or as if the suffering of others has nothing to do with the quality of our own lives.

If we are to overcome generational curses, we must recognize first that we affect each other's lives deeply. The negative things we do or fail to do have devastating effects on the lives of those who come after us. The lives we live now are strongly influenced by the lives of those who came before us. In my studies and work, I have found most often that the problems of one generation stem from the problems of the previous generation. Most of us are not living as God wants us to live. The reason is that those before us did not live as God wanted them to live. The consequences of that choice are the frustration, depression, pain, stress, confusion, dissatisfaction; irritation and weakness many of us feel in our lives. This generational trauma and disobedience is also the root cause of the self-destructive behaviors we and our family members struggle with—the overeating, the gambling, the psychosis, the pornography addictions, the abusive behaviors, anger, the drinking and drug addictions. In addition, this is the cause of many of the illnesses our loved ones and we manifest— the diabetes, heart disease, cancer, HIV, and other stress-related degenerative diseases.

This cycle of repeated failure can stop with the generation that decides to turn back to God and follow his way. Notice what God says to Cain in the story above, *"If you had done the right thing, you would be smiling; but because you have done evil, sin is crouching at your door. It wants to rule you, but you must overcome it."* Sister, please understand that Sin's goal is to rule your life and keep you and your family from joy and fulfillment. God told Cain that sin wanted to "rule him." This means to command him as a slave. However, God told Cain that, instead, Cain had to "rule over" sin. Certainly, we have seen sin rule some of our loved ones as slaves. Many of us have been ruled ourselves.

Nevertheless, I am here to tell you that you can break the generational curse in your family and protect your children and your children's children from its power. I am a witness to the power of God to do miracles in people's lives. I have seen God work in mine. He has helped me overcome multiple generational curses and break the control they had over my family's life. If you apply the same disciplines, God will do the same for you.

Throughout this book, I will share my life story and the stories of those I have met along the way as illustrations of the principles I will be teaching you. Sister, please know that this is not easy for me. The transparency necessary at times makes me feel embarrassed. But I know that my willingness to share my pain will help free some woman or girl, some husband or son, from the grip of generational curses. I am not promising the process of applying these disciplines will be easy. What I am promising is that if you have the courage to apply them, you will break the hold of any curse over your life and break free into a new relationship with God and a new experience of freedom.

God's Word: 2 Timothy 1:7: "*For God has not given us a spirit of fear and timidity, but of power, love and self-discipline.*"

To live in that freedom and to know God in that way IS your purpose in life. In the same way that you do not want your children to live in slavery, addiction, weakness, fear or self-doubt, God does not want any of his children to live in such bondage either. The problem is that change is scary. So often, the reason we do not do better is simply because we fear change. In fact, the very power that many curses hold over us is created by the fear of change itself, which reminds me of a story that illustrates my point.

In the movie *The Shawshank Redemption*, the narrator, Red, is a character wonderfully portrayed by Morgan Freeman. Red is an inmate who ends up serving nearly forty years in prison. As he tells the story, many men who live that long in bondage grow accustomed to prison life—having things provided, being told where to go and what to do, and not having independent responsibilities for themselves. In fact, Red says, they fear release, because the outside world has changed so much from when they were last there. In addition, they are older and no longer able to work the types of jobs they may have known before. In today's world, the technology has increased so dramatically in just the last ten years that it could be overwhelming for those imprisoned or out of the work force for even short periods.

As Red narrates, we learn the story of the Shawshank Prison librarian. He was an older inmate, nearly 70, when he was finally released. The prison found him a job in a grocery store and he found himself all alone. The combination of losing not only his relationships with all the other inmates and his daily routine, but also his high position as the prison librarian, where he was revered for his intelligence and power, left him despondent and hopeless. As Red tells the story, the old librarian committed suicide by hanging himself in his single room after scratching his name in the rafter above.

When Red is finally released many years later, he gets the same job at the same grocery store. Indeed, he even gets the same room and, when he enters it, sees the librarian's name still etched in the rafter above his head. The question for Red and all of us glued to the screen is *Will Red take the same path the librarian took?*

We watch Red follow the same routine as the librarian. We see the same unfamiliarity, pain and loneliness. But Red has something the librarian did not have. Red has a postcard from is friend, Andy Dufrene, the only man who ever escaped Shawshank Prison, and the central character of the movie—a man wrongly imprisoned for a murder he did not commit. Andy remembered that Red protected and befriended him in prison and helped him get everything he needed to escape. The card is an invitation to Red to not give in to despair, but to take the risk of change. It is an invitation to believe. It will not be easy for Red to follow Andy's instructions. Red must remember decade-old conversations, follow directions closely, and most of all... BELIEVE. He must believe that Andy is a man of his word. He must believe that Andy left money where he said he left it (buried beneath a tree in a field at the end of a stone wall). He must believe that he will be able to get out of the state safely, cross the border to Mexico and find Andy. In addition, he must believe that Andy will still be there as he promised.

If you have seen the movie, you know that Red finds Andy where he promised—on a beautiful beach on the coast of Mexico, just like Andy said. Rather than suicide, Red chose better and his life was renewed. He rejoins his friend, but this time in freedom.

And the misery of his captivity in Shawshank becomes a rapidly fading memory and a metaphor for us all.

For those of us under generational curses, we are like Red. Andy is like the Lord Jesus Christ—he knows our pain and he has broken the evil tyranny of the devil. In the case of Shawshank, the devil was the corrupt warden who got rich off the inmates' slave labor and kept Andy imprisoned even though he knew him to be innocent. My sister, Jesus knows your pain personally. He does not want you living in bondage, fear, depression, weakness or misery. He wants you at peace, full of joy, manifesting all that you desire in your life. And he has given you the map. He has paid the price and left instructions for you to follow to find your freedom. It is now up to you to BELIEVE and to put the work in.

God's Word: James 2:20: *"Can't you see that faith without deeds is useless?"*

Belief by itself is not enough. Red could easily have believed Andy was on the beach in Mexico waiting for him. However, that does not mean that Red would do everything he needed to do to get there. Red had to want to change.

God's Word: John 5:1-9:

"Afterward Jesus returned to Jerusalem for one of the Jewish holy days. Inside the city, near the Sheep Gate, was the pool of Bethesda, with five covered porches. Crowds of

sick people—blind, lame, or paralyzed—lay on the porches. One of the men lying there had been sick for thirty-eight years. When Jesus saw him and knew he had been ill for a long time, he asked him, "Would you like to get well?"

"I can't, sir," the sick man said, "for I have no one to put me into the pool when the water bubbles up. Someone else always gets there ahead of me."

Jesus told him, "Stand up, pick up your mat, and walk!"

Instantly, the man was healed! He rolled up his sleeping mat and began walking!"

Jesus asked the question of the crippled man near the pool of Bethesda. People believed the waters at the natural spring had the ability to heal. But they believed the waters only healed the first person to touch them whenever they bubbled up. This crippled man had been coming to the well for thirty-eight years. When Jesus met him he asked what appeared to be a very strange and even cruel question, *"Would you like to get well?"*

Here was a man who had been unable to walk, unable to care for himself and dependent on begging for a living, yet Jesus asked him if he *wanted* to be healed. What kind of question was that? Who would not want to be healed? However, what Jesus' question revealed is a deep truth of psychology. People can become very comfortable in their bondage. Even a crack house can become a place of comfort and contentment. People become comfortable with not having to be responsible for their lives. We can get used to being dependent. We can learn to love addiction, weakness, self-pity, abuse. Some of us women are so damaged that we do not believe a man loves us unless he is beating us. Some of us even deliberately do things to provoke an attack so we can be reassured of this "love."

"I can't, sir," the sick man said, "for I have no one to put me into the pool when the water bubbles up. Someone else always gets there ahead of me." Jesus' question went to the man's heart. For years, the man stayed by that well. Someone took him there every day. He knew people there. He had a social circle there. In the thirty-eight years he had been coming, it seems impossible that he had never been able to make it to the water first. Perhaps the man was comfortable with the life he lived. He obviously was not laying right on the edge of the pool waiting so that all he had to do was fall in. However, his answer revealed to Jesus that he really did desire healing.

Sister, I must ask you to look inside of your heart and answer this question: Do you desire healing? Do you want to be made whole? Or are you comfortable in your bondage? The fact that you are reading this book indicates that you desire change. But your reading the book is kind of like the man going to the healing pool. Perhaps you are reading this because your church decided to do a study on it. Perhaps you are reading it because you thought it might be interesting or someone gave you this book as a gift. The fact that you are reading this does not mean you desire healing. Everything you need is here, but there is something more you must do.

"Jesus told him, "Stand up, pick up your mat, and walk!"

Here was a man who had not walked in many years. Jesus was suddenly telling him that if he truly wanted to be healed, he needed to do something that seemed impossible. He had to take action. The man had to act on his belief. The man knew Jesus to be a healer. Jesus was telling him to demonstrate his faith by acting on Jesus' word. In the same way that Andy had invited Red to work to get to paradise, Jesus invited this man to work to receive his healing.

However, look at this, my sister, Jesus did not just tell him to do one seemingly impossible thing, Jesus told the man to do THREE seemingly impossible things: 1. *Stand up.* 2. *Take up your mat.* 3. *AND WALK.* The man could have stopped believing at any one of those things, but here is the key—once he decided to try the first thing, he was instantly healed. That is all I am asking of you as you go through this book with me. Just decide you are going to do it and you will find your healing.

What if the man did not try to get up? What if the man had waited on Jesus to pick him up? What if the man had decided that, because the healing involved work, he was not going to do it? What if the man simply did not believe Jesus? What if he thought Jesus was mocking him—telling him to do something impossible? In that case, he may well have died many years later right in that same place.

Jesus will not force healing on you. Jesus will not do the work you must do. There is a psychological reason behind this. You, and only you, must make the decision to break the generational curses in your own life. Jesus has provided the way, but you must take the action because following Christ is not a walk in the park. It is a set of disciplines that require a serious and focused mind. What took years and years to destroy in your family line is not something that will fix easily. You must not only believe, but you must take up your mat and walk. You must follow the directions and you must trust that you will reach the freedom you desire.

Why?

Because our inability to overcome our circumstances rests largely on the existence of attitudes and beliefs that hinder our options and lead us to a life of failure. These negative, weak, dependent attitudes and beliefs are what led previous generations before us into bondage. Knowing that this is not God's will for our families and that WE are responsible to change it as part of our purpose in life is central to our deliverance.

Sister, no Prince Charming is going to come to the rescue. Believe me when I tell you that no one else is going to fix your life for you. No man. No child. No lottery. Jesus is here to help you, but he is not here to live in your place. He created you to live in power—not to be a passive observer of your own life.

Purpose. Power. Life. Joy. Fulfillment. Calling. God created you to possess them all. God designed you to be the hero of your own life. Jesus is your guide. My sister, if you believe it, take up your mat and walk with me now.

CHAPTER 2

WHY IS THIS HAPPENING?
WHAT AM I DOING AND WHY?

"This kind of spirit can be forced out only by prayer." ~Mark 9:29

Because you are still reading, I trust you have decided to take up your mat and walk with me. I certainly hope so. You will not regret it. However, before we begin, I must warn you that this is a very delicate point in our journey. Right now, you are making a decision. The moment you make a decision, you will feel two things—the first will be a sense of relief that you are beginning down a path you know you should follow. This feeling is a good emotion. You are looking forward to the deliverance and freedom that will be yours the more you follow this path. You feel excited because you know a change is coming.

The second emotion is one that everyone encounters along with any decision to make a change for the better. It can take a disguise in many forms: self-doubt, frustration, anxiety, fear—any number of negative emotions that try to tell you that what you are about to do will not work. It's almost as if you can hear a little voice inside your mind that claims to know you on a much deeper level. It's a universal feeling—almost like the little devil and little angel sitting on opposite shoulders whispering both positive and negative thoughts into your ears. Right here, right now, I want to explain to you what that voice is—and please know that it doesn't matter what form it takes. Do not be deceived by that voice, whatever it is saying, whether it's telling you: that your life won't be any fun; that you're not going to finish; that you are wasting your time; that this will never work; that God isn't real, doesn't love or care for you, or won't help you, because you are worse than others or you don't deserve it. That voice is nothing more than one thing. This one thing manages to take the form of all types of feelings and thoughts and energies. But it doesn't matter what name you give it—whether you call it fear, doubt, procrastination, negativity, self-hate, weakness, or even the devil—it is still one thing. I want you to stop right now and meet this thing that has been plaguing you your whole life. I am going to name it and when I do, it will immediately begin to lose its power over you.

Are you ready? Are you sure? The name of the energy that you encounter whenever you try to do anything positive in your life is…RESISTANCE.

And that's all it is!

Whether you are trying to start a new exercise program or whether you are trying to stop being late to school, you face Resistance. Whether you are trying to write a book or trying to be patient with your kids, you face Resistance. Resistance is with me now as I type this page. I suddenly have a mind to go make a fresh cup of coffee. I have a desire to stop and stretch, to check my email, to do anything but keep writing. You might be facing Resistance to finish reading. Maybe you want a nap, you want something to eat, or you want to check your email? Perhaps there is a TV show on and you're missing it ("Girl don't remind me," I hear you saying.). Resistance is ever-present whenever we are moving towards improvement, change, betterment, accomplishment, growth, wisdom, power, freedom, or happiness.

Some people, particularly Christians or spiritual people, have often used the term "the Devil or Satan" when speaking of resistance. But it's not fair to yourself or true to God or the Bible to claim that Satan is personally trying to make you eat a cookie, or skip your workout, or be late to work. In most cases, the thing keeping you from practicing the disciplines you need to practice to change your life is you. And you do it by using whatever form of Resistance your mind has dreamed up in that moment.

Over the years, we get very good at talking ourselves out of things. That's why it's often said that in order for people to change really bad habits, they first have to hit "rock bottom." The reason they often have to hit rock bottom is because only at rock bottom do the lies we tell ourselves no longer matter. When you reach rock bottom, it does not matter any longer why you don't want to do what you need to do. At rock bottom, you MUST DO what you need to do to survive. You get the willpower to change at rock bottom because you can no longer afford to listen to your own excuses. You can no longer listen because those excuses don't matter. You have no choice. If you don't change, you will face more pain than you are willing to face or more pain than you can actually survive. At that moment, all excuses go out the window—resistance suddenly disappears and you do what you have to do.

I wanted to introduce you to resistance so that you take away its central power. The central power of resistance is its ability to masquerade as something important, reasonable, true, scary, painful, fearful, or as something that is protecting us from the unknown. But the fact of the matter is that resistance is none of the things it claims to be. Resistance is just what every single soul on the planet faces every single day of their lives.

Think about it like this: When a child has to go to school in the morning, she may not want to go, but because she has no choice, to borrow a phrase from many movie villains, "Resistance is futile." The child doesn't spend time thinking of excuses not to go to school, because she knows it's pointless. Now, if that child has an assignment due that she did not compete and she is afraid of getting a bad grade, she might try to fake an illness to avoid the pain of seeing her teacher. This might work once for the child, but it is not likely to work consistently. Eventually, the child learns to do homework and accepts the discipline of going to school.

That's the phrase I want you to embrace and use on yourself during our process together. Say it with me now, "Resistance is futile." When it comes to talking yourself out of the freedom you will get as you work through this book, tell yourself now, "Resistance is futile." That means that it doesn't matter what excuses you come up with, what pains or aches manifest in your body, what distractions come your way, you are absolutely committed to following this course of action and seeing the change you want to see in your life. RESISTANCE IS FUTILE because:

1. You are going to get this blessing!
2. You are going to get this breakthrough!
3. You are going to find your happiness in life!

Do you hear Resistance talking to you now? Maybe it's telling you that you should say, "If God is willing, you will have your breakthrough." If so, that's resistance masquerading as spirituality. How do I know this? **Because you already know that God is willing, so it can't be God saying that to you.**

At the pool of Bethesda, when Jesus asked the man whether he wanted to be made whole, did the man say, "If God is willing?" No. He said, "yes." By coming to this point, you have already said yes. And we already know God is willing. So there's no reason to allow your own Resistance to cause you to second-guess God's help in this ever again. God wants you free just as much as you want your child to be free. It would be crazy if your child was living in bondage and asked you if you were willing for him or her to be free, right? And so it is with you. In fact, often when we say "if God is willing," what we really mean is "if God does it for me" or "if God makes it easy." But the fact is that God is all for it. It is your own resistance that is fighting you.

But why do you resist your own decisions? Why do challenges emerge whenever you decide to do anything good? Ahh, now there's a good question. But it's not really the way it works. Here's something I want you to meditate on:

Challenges exist all the time.

It's just that when you decide to do something better, you pay attention to them because your mind is no longer in the routine it was in that allowed challenges to go unnoticed. Let me give you an example from my own life.

Years ago, when I first learned about the plight of poor women and children starving to death in Ethiopia, my heart ripped open and I knew I had to do something about it. Sometimes you hear stories that affect you in such a way that you cannot just let the story pass you without getting involved. That was my situation. I heard a radio interview with a representative from World Vision. In the interview, he mentioned that children in Ethiopia were starving to death. He said that children from the ages of seven to ten would organize themselves into bands of ten and go out to find food. They would live on grass and insects and when they used the bathroom, they would pass blood. After time, they would become dehydrated and World Vision would gather them by groups, put them in makeshift tents and intravenously feed them for two weeks. At the end of the two weeks, they would let them go and start all over again with another group of children.

When I heard the story, I literally screamed in my living room. I couldn't imagine that children lived like that in this world. I had come from the Caribbean and I was poor, but I'd never heard of anything like that in my life. What was most appalling was that I knew that the New York Public Schools where I worked threw away thousands of gallons of milk and thousands of pounds of food every single day of the year. I wished that there were a way I could gather all that food and send it to those children.

I began to pray daily for God to send someone to help the children in Ethiopia. One morning on my commute to work, I was praying and I felt I heard God say, "Why don't you go?" The voice was so vivid that I had to turn around to make sure I was alone. However, as I thought about it over the next few miles, I started to realize that I could do it. I paused a while as the idea marinated in my mind. I had just set up this very extensive training program for learning-disabled children that had been a huge success. If I could do that, I began to believe I could feed children in Ethiopia as well. Once I got home, I prayed about it more and decided that the minimum people would need to survive was Bread and Soup. So I called my project "The Bread and Soup Project."

The fact that, at that time, I had yet to even see an Ethiopian person before in my life didn't stop me. I didn't know if they were black, yellow or white. I just knew I had to do something. So I went on the Internet to find an Ethiopian community. Eventually, I located a pastor here in America who led me to another pastor who lived in Ethiopia. I decided to raise money for Ethiopia by organizing a concert and inviting different musicians and speakers to attend. The concert's success led me to eventually travel to Ethiopia myself and see the suffering first hand. The children were so beautiful and kind. Even though they had nothing, they wanted to give me gifts of the little trinkets they made to sell to people for money. My work with them and creating the ministries I've since created to help poor mothers and children displaced by famine, war and HIV/AIDS has been a tremendous blessing to my life, but the resistance I faced before making any of it happen is the main reason I bring all this up in this book.

Nearly as soon as I began this life changing work, I was met with issue after issue that threatened to derail my efforts. Initially, resistance met me with self-doubt. It took weeks of prayer before it ever even entered my mind that I could do anything about it myself. Why?

As I write this, there are communities in Chicago on the news that are being destroyed by gun violence. People fear walking in their own neighborhoods, because they believe they may be shot and killed in crossfire. Yet, in the midst of all this fear, there are a few people who are standing up. Why so few? If the whole neighborhood stood up, this wouldn't be a problem anymore. My belief is that many people are just as I was at the beginning—they don't even see themselves as having any power whatsoever to control the circumstances in their own lives. But as more people stand up, they slowly begin to realize they have power, too. Self-doubt is both the initial and most subtle way resistance manifests itself in our lives. We don't realize we're giving into resistance though because we haven't really made any decisions. The only thing we've done is stated a dissatisfaction—shaken our heads at the tragic news, called out "Oh, Jesus" when we heard the sad report. Many of us just mumble, "Mmm, mmm, mmm, what's the world coming to?" and change the channel because it is just overwhelming to us. Some of us put a bit more effort into it by actually praying about it. In that sense, we feel we have some power in asking God to help.

Your initial response is a gauge as to how much you care about an issue. Sometimes you care a lot. Sometimes not so much. For instance, if you hear that someone was shot in a faraway neighborhood, you may respond with the "mmm, mmm, mmm, so sad." But if you hear it was your neighborhood, you might be moved more to pray. Moreover, if you hear it was one of your friend's children, you might pray and do even more. If, God forbid, it was one of your own relatives, you would most likely be moved to take action after all the prayer—march, protest, petition for changes in the laws, start an anti-gun group, serve on neighborhood watch, or do whatever you possibly could to ensure change happens immediately.

The different reactions you have are based mostly on the proximity to your own life. In other words, your reaction is based on how much you feel an immediate threat to yourself. When you feel an immediate threat, your natural reaction is to restore safety and balance. If the threat is far away or mild, you might prioritize other things—the TV show you're missing, the work you have to do, etc. Our worlds are so busy, it's hard to care about everything. But when the threat is imminent, other issues fade in comparison.

In one case, you may think there's nothing you can do—it's far away; I don't know those people; they are foreigners or strangers, or it's happening in another part of the world and doesn't concern me. But when it's close, you have to do something. Resistance can subtly present itself in the form of self-doubt, distance, strangeness, otherness, but when it's close to you, all of that vanishes and that's when your mind may begin to seek stronger forms of resistance.

Initially, I thought there was nothing I could do but pray. But as I prayed more and more I came under the conviction that I needed to do something about it myself. At that point, resistance attacked by telling me it was a big project and I didn't know anything about the people of Ethiopia. To overcome that, I had to go online to learn about Ethiopia. I had to contact pastors and those who did know about Ethiopia and I had to sit at their feet to learn what I was missing.

You see how it worked? It started subtly with self-doubt—"I can't do anything but pray." Then I realized I could do more. Then I faced a new resistance—ignorance. So I had to overcome it with education. You can imagine what came next, right? Just think about anything you've ever done or tried to do in your life. At each phase, you face a test. At each phase, you face resistance to your goal or desire. That's how life works. That's how anything worth attaining is attained.

After my ignorance was overcome with education, I faced the obstacles that seemed more outside myself. I needed to rent a hall for the concert I decided to organize. Each venue I approached wanted something I didn't have. Most wanted a million dollar liability policy. Others wanted to charge me so much to use the place that I wouldn't have any money left to send the children. Even some of the choirs I arranged to sing charged me $2,500.00 and did not help with the tickets sales. We had to cancel because it was not financially feasible to have the choir. They kept $250.00 of our $500.00 down payment. You might want to call this form of resistance "logistical resistance." It feels like it's outside of you, but if you really look at it, it's not.

Logistical resistance is all about what you think each obstacle you come across means. It's inside of you because you are the one who determines that meaning. If four or five venues decide they want a policy I do not have, then I could either decide that means I have to stop or that it means I have to keep looking. Do you see how logistical resistance is inside of you?

I think of a friend of mine who is a salesman. He once told me a story of how his business is determined almost completely by how many people he calls on the phone. He makes phone calls to try to get people to do business with him and usually gets a no. Over the years, he calculated that for every 100 people who say no, he gets one person who says yes. That one person's business is usually worth at least $10,000. He tells the people who work under him, who are often discouraged by all the no responses they receive, that they need to change how they see the "No." "If one person in 100 earns us $10,000," he tells them, "then you have to call 100 people to make $10,000. If you divide $10,000 by 100, you get $100 per person. That means every person who tells you no is worth $100. So when you call and they say 'no,' smile and say, 'Thank you very much for helping me make $100.'" Do you see how that change in attitude overcomes any and all rejection on the phone? It doesn't matter if the person on the phone cusses and yells or screams, the salesperson is only looking for the one who says "yes."

That is true for overcoming any and every form of logistical resistance—whether you need a job, or a loan, or a donor, or a location, or a buyer, or just an opportunity. If you keep trying, keep asking, keep looking, you will eventually find the right key to open the treasure you are seeking. It's even in the Bible:

God's Word: *Luke 18:1-8: Jesus used this illustration with his disciples to show them that they need to pray all the time and never give up. ² He said, "In a city there was a judge who didn't fear God or respect people. ³ In that city there was also a widow who kept coming to him and saying, 'Give me justice.'*

⁴ "For a while the judge refused to do anything. But then he thought, 'This widow really annoys me. Although I don't fear God or respect people, ⁵ I'll have to give her justice. Otherwise, she'll keep coming to me until she wears me out.'"

⁶ The Lord added, "Pay attention to what the dishonest judge thought. ⁷ Won't God give his chosen people justice when they cry out to him for help day and night? Is he slow to help them? ⁸ I can guarantee that he will give them justice quickly."

Here we have the Lord Jesus Christ himself teaching a lesson about not giving in to resistance. It's interesting that the woman's issue is not named in the story. If her issue related to her neighbor, sister, or something specific, then we might be tempted to miss Jesus' message. The woman's issue is not relevant to what Jesus is teaching us in this story. The issue that is relevant is the woman's action when faced with resistance. What was her action when she faced the judge's resistance? SHE KEPT COMING BACK TO HIM ASKING AGAIN AND AGAIN.

The judge in this story does not want to be bothered with the woman's issue. Notice that it also doesn't matter why the judge doesn't want to be bothered It doesn't matter if he has a good reason or a bad reason, if he's just lazy or if he's corrupt. Jesus merely indicates that the judge was dishonest and did not fear God nor man, which means he obviously felt no need to honor the pledge he made as a judge before God and witnesses when he was sworn into his position of authority. He wasn't doing his job. All that matters is that he did not want to do what he was supposed to do, which was hear the woman's case and give her the justice she sought from him. He likely ignored people's needs all the time. He didn't care about the woman or his role and responsibility. But notice that it doesn't matter why he didn't care; it only matters that he didn't do anything for the woman.

But the woman persisted in asking, and that did matter. That mattered a lot. The woman's persistence eventually made even the unjust judge do right. Her persistence broke down the judge's resistance. And the same is true for you:

Your Persistence Will Break Down Resistance

When you persist in your actions, you will eventually break down whatever resistance stands against you and you will achieve the goal you want to achieve. Sometimes you find that resistance is something outside yourself—like the venues I approached that required me to give them a million dollar liability policy I did not have. Other times you find that resistance is inside of you—like self-doubt, fear, or a lack of knowledge. If you want to achieve the goal, you will prevail.

So far, my sister, we have discussed resistance as it appears in rather innocent forms. But now I want to talk a bit about resistance when it manifests in ways that threaten to destroy your sanity.

There are times when resistance manifests itself in such a powerful way that you can't help but call it Satanic. This is the type of resistance that threatens to drive you crazy, makes you feel like you want to die, and pushes you so close to the edge that you consider jumping. When you face this type of resistance, it's tempting to hurt someone else or give up by hurting yourself through drug or alcohol abuse. At the very least, this type of resistance can cause you to act pretty crazy. Let me tell you what I mean by sharing my story.

Around the same time that I decided to begin my mission to help feed children in Ethiopia, I learned that my husband was having an affair with a woman I considered one of my best friends. The pain I experienced when I learned this was deeper than any pain I'd ever experienced in my life. Although I intend to spare you all the gory details, I will share this one story to help explain how far outside of myself this resistance nearly pushed me.

After dropping my son off at the barbershop on Saturday morning, I was on my way back home when I came to a red light. While I was waiting for the light to turn green, my husband drove by with my friend in the car. They didn't get very far before my light turned green and I took off down the street behind his car. He noticed me, sped off to the shop where we have our cars serviced, and then drove off again. When I caught up with him, he pulled into the hospital parking lot and stopped. I asked him why she was with him and he lied and said she wasn't. In fact, she had gotten out of the car somewhere and I had missed it.

I got back in my car and drove back to the service shop to see if she was there. When I walked into the shop, everyone nervously watched me. The receptionist was at the front desk, two other men were standing to her right about five feet away and the owner, who always greeted me by name, just stood there frozen. My husband had dropped her off. She had run into the shop and they were now hiding her behind the counter. My heart raced as my fury grew.

I left, but I decided not to go home, because I was certain she was in the shop. I drove two blocks away and waited for her to come out.

She came out when she thought the coast was clear and drove right past my car. I followed her. She recognized I was behind her and she made a left turn, but it was too late. I was on her. My mind catapulted out of control. I smashed the gas pedal intending to crash my van into her car—but the van did not go forward. I pumped the pedal harder, but my car would not move any faster. We drove about six blocks and she came to a stop at an intersection. I tried to ram her car, but the van wouldn't do it. It was as if someone was pushing back against my foot. The van even began to stop behind her despite my foot being all the way down on the pedal.

It was not until later that night that I realized that God was watching over me. If it were up to me, she would have been dead or in the hospital and probably me along with her. I began to cry out to God in prayer.

That night, at two o'clock in the morning, I was walking around my dining room asking God to help me do better. I asked God why this was happening to me? What came into my spirit was, "You are ignorant, that's why." I stopped and responded, "But I'm educated." Then I realized that I was emotionally ignorant. I did not know how to behave in an age-appropriate way. Resistance had manifested in my marriage and life in such a way that my response was to nearly kill myself and another person. I felt helpless to change. At that point, I knew only God could help me change. So I cried out to Him in my dining room in the wee hours of the morning. I prayed, wept, and begged God to help me.

There's a story from the Bible that lines up with this experience as well. It's found in the book of Mark.

God's Word*: Mark 9:14-29: ¹⁴When they came to the other disciples, they saw a large crowd around them. Some scribes were arguing with them. ¹⁵All the people were very surprised to see Jesus and ran to welcome him. ¹⁶Jesus asked the scribes, "What are you arguing about with them?" ¹⁷A man in the crowd* *answered, "Teacher, I brought you my son. He is possessed by a spirit that won't let him talk. [18]Whenever the spirit brings on a seizure, it throws him to the ground. Then he foams at the mouth, grinds his teeth, and becomes exhausted. I asked your disciples to force the spirit out, but they didn't have the power to do it." [19]Jesus said to them, "You unbelieving generation! How long must I be with you? How long must I put up with you? Bring him to me!"[20]They brought the boy to him. As soon as the spirit saw Jesus, it threw the boy into convulsions. He fell on the ground, rolled around, and foamed at the mouth. [21]Jesus asked his father, "How long has he been like this?" The father replied, "He has been this way since he was a child. [22]The demon has often thrown him into fire or into water to destroy him. If it's possible for you, put yourself in our place, and help us!" [23]Jesus said to him, "As far as possibilities go, everything is possible for the person who believes." [24]The child's father cried out at once, "I believe! Help my lack of faith." [25]When Jesus saw that a crowd was running to the scene, he gave an order to the evil spirit. He said, "You spirit that won't let him talk, I command you to come out of him and never enter him again." [26]The evil spirit screamed, shook the child violently, and came out. The boy looked as if he were dead, and everyone said, "He's dead!" [27]Jesus took his hand and helped him to stand up. [28]When Jesus went into a house, his disciples asked him privately, "Why couldn't we force the spirit out of the boy?" [29]He told them, "This kind of spirit can be forced out only by prayer."*

This story indicates the most severe forms of resistance we face in our lives and gives us a number of insights into the nature of the strongest resistances we face. Prior to this story, Jesus had given his disciples authority to cast out demons and do miracles as he had done. The disciples had gone about town and were successful in many places. But then a man brought his son to them and they were not able to do anything. The child suffered from a spirit that hindered his speech and caused him to harm himself—often throwing himself onto the ground or into fire.

That's kind of how I felt the day I chased my husband through our town. When I walked into that service station, I was so furious I could hardly speak. And when I finally saw my former friend drive away, I was ready to throw myself into the fire—hurt myself while trying to hurt her.

Some of you reading this know all too well what I'm talking about and what it feels like to lose control over your own body and mind. Some of you experienced this feeling because of drug or alcohol abuse and some of you, like me, experienced it because of pain, rage, extreme sadness, depression, or extreme anxiety.

Another thing we learn from this story is that the young man had this spirit since he was a boy. That's what the point of this book is about—breaking bad habits and behaviors that have been ingrained in us sometimes from birth. So many times, we react to things without even thinking about them. When I saw my husband and my best friend in the car together, my mind went on autopilot. I wasn't thinking about what I was doing; I was simply reacting. I didn't think about the consequences of my actions any more than my husband or friend thought about the consequences of theirs. If God had not intervened, I doubt very seriously that I would be writing this book for you now. It was ingrained in me to act in a way that allowed my emotions to overcome me.

If you've been there before, you know what I mean. Resistance sometimes comes at us unexpectedly and with such a malicious fury that it's hard to just keep standing—let alone put up a good fight against it. You can sometimes feel like you're suffocating under the weight of the dilemma and all you want to do is breathe or scream, cry or holler or run away or die. Sometimes you just want to throw yourself into the fire.

The good news is that Jesus says that even resistance at this level is not beyond his ability to heal. And just like the previous time we looked at a scene involving Jesus healing, here again he begins with a question. We see the father told Jesus how dangerous the spirit was to the boy and then said, "If it's possible for you, please put yourself in my place and help us." He was asking Jesus to have mercy on his son. He was asking him to empathize. The father just wanted someone to understand what he and his family had been going through for so many years.

Generational issues and severe resistance can feel very isolating. Perhaps you've come to this book looking for someone to just feel what you're feeling and let you know you're not alone. Well, my sister, you are not alone. These types of feelings are common to everyone whether we hear about them or not. Jesus understands and he is willing not only to put himself in your place, but he is willing to help you also.

And that's exactly what Jesus told the man, "As far as possibilities go, all things are possible for the person who believes." Does that sound familiar? It should. It's almost the same thing he said to the man by the pool when he told him to stand up, take his mat and walk. But listen to the answer of the father. This is one of my favorite verses in the entire Bible because it demonstrates the true heart of the struggling believer. The man answered by saying, "I believe. Help my lack of faith."

Such honestly is rare for almost everyone except those who have come to the end of their ropes. It's another reason why so many have to hit "rock bottom" before they change. Sometimes it takes hitting rock bottom to get honest with yourself. The man believed, but he also recognized that he didn't completely believe.

Is that where you are right now as you begin this journey? You believe, but you have doubts. That's okay. Jesus understands. He's not asking you to be perfect; he's asking you to be willing. Willing to trust him. Willing to try. Willing to believe. He is more than happy to help your lack of faith when you are weak.

Finally, once the disciples got Jesus alone in private, they asked him a very interesting question, "Why weren't we able to force this spirit out?" Jesus' answer is powerful as well, "This kind of spirit can be forced out only by prayer." I know this intimately having found myself praying in the dining room of my home the night after my chase through our town. There are times when resistance pushes against you so hard, there is nothing you can do but pray. The good news is that PRAYER WORKS. When you pray, there is someone listening who is more than willing to help.

That night in my dining room, I prayed. It took some time, but God finally revealed to me the answer that I sought from him to help me become more emotionally mature and wise and to better overcome the strong satanic resistance I was facing in my marriage. My sister, the answers I got from that night are all in this book. By the time you finish this journey, you will have those answers as well. So hang in there with me. I'm so happy you've made it this far.

The final truth I want to share with you before we finish this chapter is that there are two very strong motivators that control the actions of every person on earth. Whether you are a saint or a sinner, these two powers are the reasons behind your actions. Sometimes when we find ourselves stuck in a rut or feeling over-powered by the resistance we face, one of these motivators is in conflict with our stated goal or desire and is the reason why we're having such a hard time. These two motivators or forces are most simply described as PAIN and PLEASURE. More specifically, there is the desire to AVOID PAIN and the desire to EXPERI-ENCE PLEASURE in our lives.

When I use the word pleasure, what I mean is anything that makes you feel good. Material things like having a job that makes money feels good. So does having a nice home, a nice car, and new clothes. Being in love gives you pleasure. So does feeling loved, feeling important, cherished, valued, appreciated. Personal achievements can give you pleasure—earning your degree, being promoted, or being honored in front of peers at work. Spirituality can give you pleasure—feeling righteous, respected, holy, and forgiven. Charity can give you pleasure—helping people, giving to needs, and contributing your time or resources. Sex and drugs can give you pleasure—from caffeine in a cup of coffee to the heroin in a dirty needle—pleasure takes many forms. Some of these forms are good, some not so good, some downright horrible for us in the long run, but in the moment, they can make you feel good.

Likewise, pain is a very strong motivator as well. But unlike pleasure, our relationship with pain is generally one of avoidance. People will do nearly anything to avoid pain—even things that lead to much more pain in the long run. Whether it's driving the speed limit so you don't get a ticket, going to church so you don't feel guilty or upset your mother, going to college so you don't end up unemployed, working very hard so you don't end up homeless, poor, or lose your car, your savings, or your position in the world; we do all types of things to avoid experiencing pain in our lives.

But the problem that we face as we try to balance our desire for pleasure against our desire to avoid pain is that we often find ourselves in conflict. So many times, we have to endure short-term pain in order to gain the pleasure later. This is commonly called delayed gratification. Our mind often fights against us as we try to face the pain of studying in order to pass the test, get the grade, pass the class, get the degree and get the job. The further away the pleasure is, the harder it is to endure the pain that we must overcome first.

On top of this, our society conditions us for the opposite of delayed gratification. Almost everything in our society is designed not for delayed gratification but for instant gratification. Drive the car now; pay for it when? Later. Buy the clothes now; pay for it when? Later. Have the fun now; pay for it when? Later. Everywhere we turn we're offered easy pleasures to enjoy. Marketing people know this is the key to getting people to buy—make it cheap, fast, easy and fun. If you have to tell the price at all, do so in as tiny a print as possible. The new car you want is only $300/month (when you put $5000 down and don't drive it more than 10,000 miles a year and return it after 4 years of on-time payments in excellent condition and have excellent credit and more fine print). YELL THE PLEASURE. Whisper the pain. The combo meal at your favorite fast-food restaurant might cost only $6.99, until you factor in how much you might spend in medical bills having your heart treated later. It's fine to eat on occasion, but eating there regularly will cost you far more in the long run. Likewise, a hit of some illegal drug might feel amazing for a short time, but do unimaginable damage over time.

We're exposed to so much marketing that we easily come to expect everything in life to be like buying something on credit. Some sociologists have come to describe our culture as the microwave generation—we want what we want and we want it fast and easy. But the best things in life don't come like that. The best things in life generally have to be planted at the right time, nurtured carefully and harvested after long seasons. That's one reason you can't find any restaurants touting their wonderful microwave menu.

Most experts agree also that the strongest of the two motivators is our desire to avoid pain. In most cases, the desire to avoid pain is much stronger than the desire to gain pleasure. When one action achieves both goals, it is understood as an easy choice, easy decision or easy action. But when there is conflict between pain and pleasure, you experience resistance. And it is your responsibility to recognize this in every area of your life.

Let me give you an example. Many people desire to lose weight. People see ads for workout machines or exercise programs on TV and order them every chance they get. But most people who order these things from TV either never use them or only use them once or twice before quitting. This is a very clear example of the power of pain and pleasure at work in our lives. Here's how: The ad is sold with images and videos of people with perfect bodies telling you how great the machine or program is. You imagine yourself looking like the models on TV and you want to believe it. You want to be happy like they are. You want to feel good about your body like they do. The testimonials convince you it's possible, so you order the program. You excitedly anticipate the package's arrival. When it comes you put it together or pop it in the DVD player and get ready for the new body. That's when you feel it for the first time. The pain. There was no real pain before this unless there was a high price, but usually it's not the price. You may even have a free at home trial. The pain is the pain of the exercise itself. Or maybe you read the plan and see that to get the results of the models on TV, you also have to change your diet. YIKES—more pain.

This is where the conflict for most of us is strongest. You want the new body (positive). You want the healthy, happy feeling (positive). You want the confidence (positive). But to get it, you have to go through some pain (negative). That pain is not only in the exercise but in the diet (negative). Most people try one or two more times before they abandon the program altogether and the DVDs or machines gather dust in a corner of the garage or basement. Why? Because the pain outweighed the anticipated pleasure for them. For a few, the pain of continuing to be out of shape is stronger than the pain of enduring the workout and they are often the ones who are successful. In general, the avoidance of pain is a stronger motivator than gaining pleasure.

But imagine this little difference. What if a person who goes to his or her doctor learns they have a condition, which will kill them if they don't start excising and change their diet NOW! What do you think their chances of success will be? Well, if they value their life and trust their doctor, they will get serious about working out at any costs. The reason is because the pain of dying is greater than the pain of exercising. In this case, the pain is working for them to help them reach their goal rather than working against them. There is little resistance when pain and pleasure are working together.

I mention this because I want you to be aware of these forces as they play out during our time together in this book. When you're tempted to quit, try to put your finger on the exact thing that resistance is telling you. What pleasure is it promising you? Or what pain is it threatening you with? If you can identify these and begin to understand them more clearly, you will find it easier and easier to fight resistance in other areas of your life as it challenges your goals and desires.

If you want to experience the best that God has for you, you have to face and overcome resistance. You will have to go through some pain to get to the pleasure that waits on the other side.

When you ask yourself, "Why is this happening to me?" understand that the reason is because you have decided to live a more abundant and powerful life. You have chosen to move forward in your relationship with God to see what all he has in store for you. Like a new soldier, you have to train yourself to fight on the new level you seek. Each time you overcome resistance, you grow stronger and wiser and closer to God. Each time you endure a short-term pain to gain a greater pleasure later, you gain a victory.

To ensure you continue to gain more victories, you have to learn to use a few weapons along the way. I'm very excited for you, my sister. You've already come so far. The sky is the limit for what God can do in your life. In the next chapter, we'll talk about your key to successfully overcoming life's difficulties and how to leverage the power of pain and pleasure to help you break completely free of generational issues that may have been plaguing you or your family for years.

Chapter 3

SYNCHRONIZING YOUR FAITH

"Faith is the substance of things hoped for, the evidence of things not seen." Hebrews 11:1

My sister, because you are a child of Jesus Christ there is something I know is true about you that you may or may not know is true. I know it because God says it is true of all of his children. It is a simple fact and there is no escaping it. As hard as it might be to believe, it is still true. Even if it doesn't feel like it is still true. What is it? What I know about you and everything that happens in your life is simply this: *Everything that happens in your life, no matter how crazy or painful or evil or hard to believe—everything in your life works together for your good.*

Did you hear that? Did you understand it? Did it make you smile? If it didn't make you smile, then you must not have either heard it, got it, or believed it. Let me write it again for you to read again. This time when you read it, I want you to say it aloud to yourself and really think about it.

"Everything that happen in my life, no matter how crazy or painful or evil or hard to believe—everything in my life works together for my good."

Really think about that. Think about "everything"—not just the good things, not just the happy things, not just the things you smile about or are proud of—think about all things. Every heartache. Every time you cried. Every loss you've endured. Every humiliation or embarrassment. Every hurt. It's not easy to bring all those things to memory, but there is one thing I know for certain about each and every one of them. No matter how they felt, no matter how much residual pain you still experience because of them. No matter how many tears you've shed or times you've felt shameful or disgusted or damaged—each and every one of those things works for your good. It's a type of magic that God does in the lives of his children. That's what it says in the book of Romans chapter 8 and verse 28. In fact, it says two things, "God makes all things work together for the good of those who love him, those who are called according to his purpose."

He MAKES all things work for our good.

Someone reading this is doubting. You're being attacked by resistance now because you might have picked up on that phrase "those who love him" and you may be asking yourself "how do I know I love him?" "How could I love God if I've done these bad things?" But the next verses clear things up for those of us who think our faith in God is based on our own power and strength. Here's the verse in context:

God's Word: *Romans 8:28-30: "28And we know that God causes all things to work together for good to those who love God, to those who are called according to His purpose. 29For those whom He foreknew, He also predestined to become conformed to the image of His Son, so that He would be the firstborn among many brethren; 30and these whom He predestined, He also called; and these whom He called, He also justified; and these whom He justified, He also glorified...."*

What that set of verses says in a nutshell is that God is in control of all things concerning his children. Not only did he know you before you were born, he chose you and already decided that you were to become like Christ way before you even knew who Christ was. Then he called you—that's why you believe in God now. Then he justified you—forgave your sins through Christ and he is now about to glorify you. In fact, it's already done, you just haven't experienced it yet. Just as it's possible to have read this verse before you came to faith, you are most likely reading it before you experience the glory that God has already done for you from his perspective. Do you see how this works? God is way ahead of us. Still a little lost? Let me try to explain it another way.

You've been to the movies and watched the story unfold on the film. When you're in a good movie you get caught up in the action and characters—the plot, setting, characters, dialog, special effects, the close calls and near misses—the moment. You are watching the film as it happens before you. But imagine if you are the director. You already know how the film ends. The director knows the ending of the film before you even begin to watch it. In fact, he knows it before you even see the previews of it. In fact, he put it together on a story board long before the actors were even hired to play the roles. God sees the film of your life on his story-board. In fact, he sees it from the script—from the beginning to the ending—he already knows the twists and turns and he knows the happy ending he has planned. He even said so in other verses before the one above.

"For I know the plans I have for you, says the Lord. Plans of peace and not of evil. Plans to give you a future and a hope." (Jeremiah 29:11)

Now you may be having some trouble with this. I understand. It's hard to see tragedies that happen in our lives as working together for our good. For some of us, it even feels wrong to believe it. It's almost as if God must be evil if he allowed this to happen to me. Sometimes the pain of an experience is so great that we can't see past it at all. We can't see how a loving God could ever allow some of the evil that has happened to people around the world. I admit, it's a very hard concept to grasp, but it is a crucial one as well.

God's perspective is eternal. Think about that. We see things from the present, as human beings trapped in time and space. We see a beginning of life and an end of life. As far as we know, what we see is all that exists for us. That's not true of God. We may only see things from our perspective, but God sees many perspectives. He views our lives from the standpoint of eternity and understands our lives in the grander scheme of his entire plan for the universe. What does that mean? It means you're reading this book for a reason. You're hearing these words for a reason. God is speaking to you now for a reason. No matter how damaged you think you are, you are actually chosen. No matter how much hurt you've endured or may still be enduring, God is letting you know right now that he has a plan for you. Your life is not over. It's not done. It's not broken beyond repair. God is here and he has you right where you're supposed to be so that he can help you be who you were meant to be.

This is a difficult concept, but it's important for you to under-stand in order to activate the key weapon in your battle against generational curses in your life and family. It's important because in order to move against the forces that have been tying you and your family down for generations, you absolutely must believe that God is with you in this journey. You must know without a doubt that you will win. It is just as the Bible says, "if God is for you, who can stand against you?" Where does it say that in the Bible? Well, it's in the very next verse of course— verse 31 of Romans chapter 28. Because God has done all these things for us—chosen us, given us faith, forgiven our sins and begun to craft us into the glorious beings he wants us to become… who can possibly stop him? The answer is assumed—NO ONE. No one can stand against what God is doing in your life. You are coming to your glory, my sister. It is part of God's miraculous plan for your life. He's gotten this far and he is unstoppable in taking you the rest of the way.

Isn't that great news? I hope there is a smile on your face as you read this, because that would mean it's sinking in. You are predestined not only to your salvation, but to your victory over anything that has been plaguing your life, frustrating your family, or hindering your path. You are chosen and backed by God Almighty himself. You can bet on yourself to win this one, because you're backed by the best, and the fix is in!

So when I talk in this chapter about synchronizing your faith, what I mean is getting your faith to line up with this reality. If you're understanding what I'm saying, you should be smiling now. The reason you're smiling should be because you understand that there's no reason not to smile. The fix is in, and you're going to win. It does not matter what your circumstances look like now. It does not matter what you've gone through or what you're going though. In the end, YOU WILL WIN! God guarantees it! Any pain and craziness you're going through now will be a distant memory soon because God is working something out in your life. That smile on your face, therefore, should be a smile of victory.

As you read this, you are synchronizing your faith to what God's word says is true. When you line your faith up with his word, you experience the power, presence and the inevitability of God's perfect will. You feel a sense of peace and joy. You feel your heart calm with the quiet of knowing you are cared for and you will be just fine. Your heart becomes light as if floating on a raft in a swimming pool without a care in the world. When you synchronize your faith with God's word and begin to believe what God says is true about you, you plug into the source of all power, joy, peace, comfort and provision.

Don't get me wrong, this doesn't mean that all your troubles cease. Synchronizing your faith is about adjusting your thoughts and bringing them in line. Remember what Jesus said about worry? He said don't do it, because *it won't add a day to your life or an inch to your height.* So often, it is the perspective we have that makes whatever we're going through easier or harder to tolerate.

Let me give you an example. Say you're late to work. If you believe that by being late to work you're going to lose your job, then not be able to pay your rent, then lose your house and then become homeless, the stress you will feel about being late will be overwhelming. But if you believe that your boss will understand and it's not that big of a deal, you likely won't be too concerned about the traffic accident that's holding you up. In fact, you might be able to even be grateful that you weren't the one in the accident.

Synchronizing your faith with God is kind of like knowing that your boss may not understand and may fire you, but somehow, someway, God is going to make things turn out for your good anyway. Perhaps you'll get a better job. Perhaps you'll start a business. Perhaps it will work out some other way. Synchronizing your faith is about living life with a positive expectation of life and the confident assurance that God is directing your steps. You can't do anything about the traffic, true. But God can. Still, he allowed you to be stuck in it this morning, so there must be a good reason. It doesn't mean you don't care about being on time—of course, you do. But what it does mean is that when negative things happen, you know and understand, without a shadow of a doubt, that things will work out for good anyway.

When you synchronize your faith with what God's word says, you choose to believe God rather than the doubts and fears that manifest themselves in your current circumstances. Doubts and fears are very strong precursors of pain. In other words, you experience doubts and fears when you anticipate pain. Think back to when you were a child and you got a splinter in your finger. If you were like me, the first time it happened you ran to your mother crying and showing her the finger that hurt. If your mom was like my mom, she took your hand and said, "Here, let me get that out, baby." And if you were like me, you yanked your hand away for fear that whatever she would do would make your hand hurt more. After some coaxing, your mom either finally got you to trust her or she made you give up the hand against your will.

Synchronizing your faith is like believing that a loving mother is going to help you instead of hurt you. If you were like me, you squirmed right up until the pain went away. You may have even screamed when you felt her tug it. But then the pain was gone.

The splinter was removed and everything was right with the world again. God is a loving father who wants us to trust him. Sometimes we mistake the splinters we get from the world as some sign that he doesn't really love us or care for us. But that's not true. Synchronizing your faith is about recognizing truth, trusting God and believing his solution is the best solution for you—even if it does look like it will hurt.

So how do we synchronize our faith?

God's Word: *Romans 10:17: "So faith comes from what is heard, and what is heard comes through the message about Christ."*

Just like a commercial that you see on TV over and over and over again before it eventually convinces you to try a product, constantly reading and rereading God's word will gradually help you trust him. The more of God's word you read, the more you realize how much it applies to your life. The more you realize it applies, the more you turn to it for guidance. The more you turn to it for guidance, the more you experience God's hand in your life. The more you experience God's hand in your life, the easier it is to trust him.

The first time you get a splinter, you may run to mommy. Once mommy pulls it out, you trust her more. In fact, you ran to her in the first place because she had proven her ability to feed, shelter, protect and comfort you in the past. The more we turn to God for help, the more help we receive and the more we are able to trust him. Reading his word daily is the best practice for helping us stay mindful that God is present in our lives and circumstances. Reading also helps us to understand that God desires us to come to him.

God's Word: *1 Peter 5:7: "Give all your worries and cares to God, for he cares about you."*

God doesn't want you to just give some of your worries and cares to him. He wants you to give ALL of your worries and cares to him. Think about that. Here is a clear invitation to live your life in the complete confidence and trust that God can handle and will handle all of your worries and cares. Worries and cares have the ability to feel exactly like a weight on our shoulders. People who study body language know that when a person is sad, depressed, worried, frustrated or overwhelmed, it shows in how they walk and sit. They actually sit as if they have a weight on their backs that forces their shoulders forward and their head down. God here is saying that he wants you to give those worries and cares to him as if you are giving him a giant backpack that has been stressing you out, weighing you down, and making every step of your life a struggle.

In fact, that's a great way to know that you have actually given your worries to God. When you are concerned with something, notice your posture. Are your shoulders curled forward? Do you look weighed down? If so, give those concerns and worries to God. If you truly do, you should notice it in your physical posture.

Your shoulders should move up and back with confidence. You should feel a sense of relief in your body. When you have truly given your backpack of worries and cares to God, you will feel lighter… relieved.

> **God's Word**: *Psalm 55: 22: "Cast your burden on the LORD, and He will sustain you; He will never allow the righteous to be shaken."*

When you're burdened by a situation and you feel over-whelmed, it can be hard to see yourself as righteous, but remember that God made you righteous through your faith in Christ. It's not about how you feel or what you've done—it's about what Jesus did on the cross. It's about truth. When you synchronize your faith to God's word, you understand that you are not on this journey alone and that God is able to carry your burden and wants to carry it. This verse can be seen in a number of different ways. Have you ever lifted a weight that was so heavy, it literally made your legs shake to hold it? When it comes to burdens, God doesn't want to see you shaking in your boots. Faith is knowing God is an ever-present source of power and strength. He will sustain you.

Another way to look at this verse is in terms of fear. Some-times fear can make us physically shake as well. Fear can be a terrible burden to bear. God invites you to cast that fear on him as well. He wants you strong and confident. Look at this verse:

God's Word*: Hebrews 13:6: "So we can confidently say, 'The Lord is my helper; I will not fear; what can man do to me?'"*

Notice how the writer of Hebrews is making a decision. He says he "will not" fear. That indicates a conscious choice in his behavior. He could fear, but he WON'T fear because he has no reason to fear. The writer of Hebrews is saying that he is synchronizing his faith to God's word and adjusting his actions accordingly. He was likely thinking of this wonderful verse from the Old Testament:

God's Word*: Psalms 27:1: "The Lord is my light and my salvation; whom shall I fear? The Lord is the stronghold of my life; of whom shall I be afraid?"*

Or better yet, maybe this one:

God's Word*: Psalms 118:6-8: "The Lord is on my side; I will not fear. What can man do to me? The Lord is on my side as my helper; I shall look in triumph on those who hate me. It is better to take refuge in the Lord than to trust in man."*

I love Psalm 118:6-8 because it's so in line with today's slang. You can interpret it to say "I will look in triumph on my haters because I care more about what God thinks than what they think." After all, haters are going to hate. Right, sister?

Do you see how spending time in God's word helps to build your faith and confidence to trust in him more and more? In fact, here's another verse that many people have memorized to make sure they remember to think of God in every situation:

God's Word: *Proverbs 3:5-6: "Trust in the Lord with all your heart and lean not on your own understanding. In all your ways acknowledge him and he will direct your path."*

The Bible is full of scriptures that encourage us to trust in God's care and concern for us. Synchronizing your faith is similar to updating the software on your computer so that it works according to the manufacturer's recommendations. Daily updates with God's word help to ensure you experience God's presence and guidance to the fullest.

Synchronizing your faith can be summed up by the Proverbs 3:5-6 verse above. When you synchronize your faith, you are trusting in the Lord instead of leaning on your own understanding. You are consciously and deliberately taking God's word and forcing your mind to focus on it as opposed to whatever other intrusive, negative, fearful, damning, hurtful and disempowering thoughts your mind might otherwise contemplate. Whether those thoughts come from some negative experience of your past or some person standing right in front of you in your present, synchronizing your faith with God's word is about ACKNOWLEDGING GOD before you allow that thought to root and definitely before you take any action. Your understanding might tell you to fear, to worry, to give up, to cuss, to kill, to hurt back, to lie, to steal, to smoke, to drink, to eat, to shoot up, to shoot someone else, to seek vengeance, or to deceive. Your mind and experiences might tell you that you're too weak, too stupid, too afraid, too ugly, too new, too female, too inexperienced, too young, too little, too big, too timid, too intimidated, too puny, or too full of negativity.

BUT NONE OF THAT MATTERS!
ALL THAT MATTERS IS: WHAT DOES GOD SAY?

Synchronizing your faith to God's word is about forcing your thoughts to adjust to the creator's thoughts about you. You may think those negative things, but God thinks you're perfect, you're smart, you're capable, you're strong, you're able, you're beautiful, you're powerful, you're saved, you're worthy, you're deserving, you're strong, you're right, you're courageous, you're good. God says you should not fear, you should trust, you should believe, you should try, you should take on the challenge, you will win, you can't lose, you can't fail.

Speaking of not being able to fail, do you know that the word "failure" does not appear anywhere in the Bible? Isn't that a wonderful truth? There is no failure in God's word.

When I decided to organize a concert for children of Ethiopia, I faced opposition from so many directions that I was tempted to just give up. So many people wanted so much money that the concert seemed as if it wouldn't raise a dime. Add to that the fact that on the day of the concert it began to rain. I wanted to call the whole thing off. But I didn't believe that God would bring me that far to leave me, so I pushed onward. The concert went off without a hitch and more people showed up than even I expected. It was a tremendous success that led me to visit the country of Ethiopia myself, and gave me the opportunity to plant a church in Nairobi and Kisii, Kenya as well as oversee another in Solai, Nakuru. We help support an orphanage in Nairobi, and a school in Solai, which has a mission to help women and children who are economically disenfranchised.

During my struggle to build these ministries, I've come to develop a five step plan for helping to ensure my faith is synchronized with God's Word.

1. The first step is to IDENTIFY THE PROBLEM OR ISSUE with which you are struggling. Make sure to write it down. It is so important that you be very clear what the issue is that you want to resolve. If you're not clear on the issue, you will have a hard time following the next step.

2. ALIGN YOUR EXPECTATIONS with God's word. This means that you seek out specific scriptures where God speaks directly to the issue or problem you are facing. This is important because you can't expect God to do something other than what he promised he'd do. I should change that—you can expect him to do something other than he promised, but that's often what

leads people to struggle with their faith. If God did not promise anything related to the issue, or if he promised to do the opposite of what you want, you can become very frustrated trying to get God to change his mind. After all, he is God and he knows what's best. So make sure that your expectations are on track with his promises.

3. MEDITATE on a particular scripture for the duration of the problem. By this, I do not mean that you do nothing else. I simply mean that you find one specific scripture related to your issue that promises you the outcome you desire. Memorize this scripture and think about it throughout the day.

4. BELIEVE that God's promise about the issue will come to pass. When you believe something, your actions tend to follow. James says, "Show me your faith by your works." If you believe, you will develop peace about it. You will relax and you will trust. Believe that God will do just what he says he will do because he will.

5. Continue to pray and believe it will happen until it does. Remember what we discussed in the last chapter—"Your persistence will overcome resistance." The temptation is to give up after some time in prayer and meditation, but the key is to keep seeking the promises

until they come to pass. I'm not sure why God chooses to require us to persist sometimes. There are times when my prayers are answered instantly and there are times when it feels like what is described in the Book of Daniel—the answer to my prayer is being held up in the heavens by powerful forces. Whatever the reason, God sometimes requires us to persevere to get the promise that he made. Again, this doesn't happen all the time, but sometimes you will feel like the man with the demon-possessed son, "Lord I believe. Help my unbelief." Still, just as Jesus did in fact help that man's unbelief, he will likewise help yours.

If you're struggling with an issue right now, you may be wondering what scriptures you can use to apply the principles I outlined above. If you have access to a computer or a smartphone, it's very easy today to find scriptures for any issue you're dealing with. Go to Google and query: "Scriptures related to: _____" In the space, type in the problem you are dealing with. For instance, type in "Scriptures related to healing" if you're worried about some illness you or a loved one is facing. Another way would be to query: "God's promises to help me deal with_____" and in the space there, put the issue you are dealing with. For example: "God's promises to help me deal with depression."

If you don't have access to a computer or smartphone, you can often find topical scriptures in the back of your Bible. If that's not true of your particular version of the Bible, you can also call your church, ask a friend or relative who has access to technology to look up some scriptures for you, or speak with your pastor. If none of these resources are available to you, below are a few scriptures for a few common issues that might also help.

TOPICAL SCRIPTURES FOR MEDITATING ON GOD'S PROMISES:

Depression: Psalm 34:18, 19: "The LORD is close to the brokenhearted and saves those who are crushed in spirit. (19) A righteous man may have many troubles, but the Lord delivers him from them all." Other scriptures for depression: Deuteronomy 31:8, Deuteronomy 33:27, 2 Samuel 22:17-22, Ecclesiastes 9:4, Psalm 9:9, Psalm 27:14, Isaiah 26:3-4, Isaiah 40:31, Philippians 4:6-7.

Forgiveness: Isaiah 1:18: "Come now, let us reason together, says the LORD: though your sins are like scarlet, they shall be as white as snow; though they are red like crimson, they shall become like wool." Other scriptures about forgiveness: Psalm 103:8-12, Matthew 5:22-24, Acts 10:42-43, 2 Corinthians 5:18-19, Ephesians 1:7-10, Colossians 1:13-14.

God's Presence in hard times: 2 Corinthians 1:10: "He delivered us from such a deadly peril, and he will deliver us. On him we have set our hope that he will deliver us again." Other promises of His presence in hard times: Psalm

66:17-20, Colossians 1:13, Hebrews 6:19-20, James 1:2-4.

Feeling Weak/Overwhelmed: Isaiah 40:28: "Have you not known? Have you not heard? The LORD is the everlasting God, the Creator of the ends of the earth. He does not faint or grow weary; his understanding is unsearchable." Other scriptures for when you feel weak or overwhelmed: 1 Samuel 2:2, Psalm 37:5, Ephesians 6:2, John 14:1, 2 Corinthians 1:3-5.

God's Sufficiency/Provision: Psalm 103:4-5: "The Lord redeems your life from destruction. He crowns you with loving-kindness and tender mercies. The Lord satisfies your mouth with good things; so that your youth is renewed like the eagle's." Other scriptures of God's sufficiency and provision: Isaiah

58:10, 2 Corinthians 3:5-6, 2 Corinthians 12:9, 1 John 4:4, 2 Corinthians 9:8, Psalm 23.

Healing: Psalm 41:3: "The LORD sustains them on their sickbed and restores them from their bed of illness." Other scriptures on God's healing: Isaiah 53:5, Psalm 30:2, Luke 8:50, Psalm 147:3.

Seeking Encouragement: My help comes from the Lord, Who made heaven and earth. He will not allow your foot to slip or to be moved; He Who keeps you will not slumber. Psalms 121:2-3. Other scriptures for when you seek encouragement: Romans 15:5, Galatians 6:2, 1 Peter 5:7, 2 Thessalonians 2:16-17, Psalm 37:7, Isaiah 51:12, Isaiah 49:13, Psalm 55:22, Psalm 46:1.

Overcoming Fear/Doubt/ Worry: Luke 24:38: "And he said to them, "Why are you troubled, and why do doubts arise in your hearts?" Other scriptures to overcome fear, doubt or worry: Mark 11:23, Hebrews 11:1-40, John 20:27, Isaiah 41:10, John 14:1, Job 23:8-10, 2 Timothy 1-7, 1 Peter 5:6-7.

Confidence: Philippians 4:13: "I can do all things through Him who strengthens me." Other scriptures to give you confidence: Hebrews 4:16, Deuteronomy 31:6, Joshua 1:9, 1 John 5:14, I Corinthians 15:58, Psalm 27:1, Psalm 55:22, 1 Samuel 17: 32-37, 2 Chronicles 32:6-7.

Overcoming Hopelessness: Romans 15:4: "For everything that was written in the past was written to teach us, so that through endurance and the encouragement of the Scriptures we might have hope." Other scriptures to help you overcome hopelessness: Romans 15:13, Ephesians 1:18-19, Psalm 37: 9, Psalm 42:5, Psalm 25:3, Matthew 11:28-30, 2 Corinthians 12:9.

Success: Habakkuk 2:3: "But these things I plan won't happen right away. Slowly, steadily, surely, the time approaches when the vision will be fulfilled. If it seems slow, do not despair, for these things will surely come to pass. Just be patient! They will not be overdue a single day." Other scriptures that promise success: John 15:16, Galatians 6:9, Proverbs 24:16, Psalms 1:1-3, Jeremiah 29:11, Joshua 1:8.

Handling Temptation: 1 Peter 4:12: "Dear friends, do

not be surprised at the painful trial you are suffering, as though something strange were happening to you." Other scriptures to help you handle temptation: 1 Corinthians 10:13, 1 Timothy 6:9, James 4:7, Galatians 5:16, James 1:14, Psalms 119:11, 1 Timothy 6:6-14, Philippians 4:13.

Loneliness: Romans 8:35-39: "Who shall separate us from the love of Christ? Shall tribulation, or distress, or persecution, or famine, or nakedness, or danger, or sword? As it is written, "For your sake we are being killed all the day long; we are regarded as sheep to be slaugh-tered." No, in all these things we are more than conquerors through him who loved us. For I am sure that neither death nor life, nor angels nor rulers, nor things present nor things to come, nor powers, nor height nor depth, nor anything else in all creation, will be able to separate us from the love of God in Christ Jesus our Lord." Other scriptures to help you overcome loneliness: Psalm 38:9, Psalm 27:10, Isaiah 41:10, Psalm 25:16, Matthew 28:20, Joshua 1:5.

Help for your Children: Matthew 18:2-6: "He called a little child and had him stand among them. And he said: "I tell you the truth, unless you change and become like little children, you will never enter the kingdom of heaven. Therefore, whoever humbles himself like this child is the greatest in the kingdom of heaven. "And whoever welcomes a little child like this in my name welcomes me. But if anyone causes one of these little ones who believe in me to sin, it would be better for him to have a large millstone hung around his neck and to be drowned in the depths of the sea." Other scriptures to help your children: Psalm 8:2, Psalm 127:3-5, Proverbs 22:6, Matthew 18;10, Proverbs 1:8-9, Mark 9:36-37.

Happiness: Psalm 37:4, "Delight yourself also in the LORD: and he shall give you the desires of your heart." Other scriptures about how to find happiness: Proverbs 16:20, Ecclesiastes 3:13, Philippians 4:4, Isaiah 26:3-4, 1 Corinthians 13:1-13, Micah 6:8.

My sister, when you read and meditate on these scriptures and many others like them, you will come to understand that all you need can be found in Jesus. I pray that you will find power and joy in applying these promises to your daily life so that you can walk in the power God has given to you.

Now that we've covered the requirements for knowing your purpose, understanding what is going on in your life, why we do what we do, and how to use God's word to help us synchronize our faith to overcome our negative thinking and actions, it is time to take a look at generational curses so that we can understand how to break them in our lives and in the lives of our loved ones.

Chapter 4

WHAT ARE GENERATIONAL CURSES?

I lavish unfailing love to a thousand generations. I forgive iniquity, rebellion, and sin. But I do not excuse the guilty. I lay the sins of the parents upon their children and grandchildren; the entire family is affected--even children in the third and fourth generations." ~Exodus 34:7

The concept of generational curses is difficult for many believers to understand and accept because it gives the impression that our loving God is vindictive, punitive and mean. However, to truly understand generational curses, we need to understand a bit about how God made man and why the actions of our parents, grandparents and great-grandparents can have effects on our lives today.

God made man a social being and he created us to pass our genes on from one generation to the next. As such, we often find that we have our ancestor's eyes, nose, hair, height, build, or other noticeable features. It's very common even for traits to skip a generation and show up in grand or great grandchildren.

We know this is also true when it comes to some diseases. If your ancestors had certain diseases, such as sickle cell anemia, cancer or heart disease, your doctor will tell you that you and others in your family are at risk for it as well. In these cases, it's important to do proper screenings and keep an eye on vulnerable areas of concern. This is just the way we are made as human beings.

Likewise, some people have a natural resistance to certain diseases. For instance, there are people who have a natural resistance to HIV. And of course, we know that if a parent was an athlete, musician, or scientist, their children often inherit certain traits that make them successful in those fields as well. A parent with a healthy physical body usually produces offspring who have few weight challenges and who seem to naturally have a good shape. And a parent who is overweight often produces offspring who struggle with weight.

Genetic science today is just beginning to understand how this works. The field of epigenetics teaches now that certain markers are turned on and off in babies based on their parents' actions before pregnancy, in vitro and after birth. These markers determine whether children become prone to anxiety, depression, disease and fear, or whether they handle stress well, are generally happy, positive people and many other things. Even tests on mice show that mothers who lick and groom their pups after birth develop healthy adult mice. Pups whose parents are kept from licking and grooming them after birth develop anxiety, poor health and die much earlier. Genetic evidence shows that certain genes get blocked or unblocked depending on how the mice pups are cared for after birth. These genes then automatically effect the mice for the rest of their lives. When they encounter stressful situations, mice with the certain genes turned on cope better and find solutions to their problems. Mice without the gene turned on, panic, stress out and fail to find solutions.

These genes can continue to be turned on or off throughout our childhood before they lock and become part of our personality. For instance, psychologists tell us that events which children experience (such as the divorce of parents or abuse) get imprinted onto the child with emotions, which is often void of words that define or express it. However, when we talk to a therapist or a pastor, we must use words to identify the emotion that was imprinted. If what was imprinted on you was a wordless emotion, it is often difficult to find words to describe it enough to identify and heal it. So much of the work of today's therapists is just trying to get clients to find the words that match the emotions they feel. So much of the frustration in therapy is the difficulty of finding words to express the pain, hurt and confusion that affects the client today.

Imagine this example: A large tree grows on your property next to your house. The tree has been growing for 30 years and is very healthy. However, you recently learned that its roots have burst through your sewer and your toilet is now backing up into your basement, which threatens your family's health. You call a plumber who rooters the pipes and tears out the roots, but since the tree is still growing, the roots return. This problem recurs every six months costing you hundreds and thousands of dollars. You must destroy the tree to fix the problem. You might hire a tree service to cut down the tree, but if they leave the stump, the roots will continue to grow and eventually the tree will return. Digging up the roots and killing the stump can cause a lot of damage to the surrounding yard—it can get ugly. On top of that, you might begin to wax nostalgic over the tree. Maybe you once built a treehouse in it for your kids or put a swing in it. Or maybe you remember that it shaded the backyard when you had barbecues. All of these things can make the decision to dig up the roots and destroy the tree very difficult. If it's difficult to dig up a tree, imagine how difficult it is to dig up the painful things that have been part of you for 20, 30, 40 or sometimes even 50 years.

In some sense, this is nothing more than playing life with the hand we get dealt. We have no choice in picking how we are born or to whom or under which circumstances, habits or challenges. In many ways, some are just luckier than others. Some of us had loving parents who were raised well, took care of themselves, planned and wanted our birth, planned for us financially, ate right, got good medical care and parental training, loved each other and loved us. However, some of us had parents who weren't prepared to be parents—they were too young, unemployed, addicted, confused, fooling around on a one night stand, drunk, high, homeless, irresponsible, uneducated, desperate, poorly raised themselves, unhealthy, and unconcerned about the little baby they brought into the world. Regardless of which parents we had, we must simply find our way to success despite our circumstances.

For many of us, circumstances can be very unfortunate. God has chosen those of us with particularly difficult circumstances to develop a unique and powerful set of skills to overcome those circumstances.

To begin to learn these skills, we must first learn what we are dealing with. That's what I want to discuss in this chapter—how generational curses manifest themselves in our lives.

Remember, by generational curses, I do not mean that God actively strikes us down. Nothing could be further from the truth. God is not at all interested in his children falling victim to any type of curse. All that I mean is that God has made mankind a certain way that allows the actions of our ancestors to impact our lives both positively and negatively.

The positive impacts of ancestral behavior, we tend to call "inheritance." You inherited your mother's wit, your father's courage, your grandmother's sense of adventure. We appreciate the positive impacts. However we'd rather not have the negative impacts. The negative impacts of ancestral behavior is what the Bible refers to as "curse." You hear someone say he was cursed with his father's taste for alcohol, cursed with his grandfather's gambling habit, or cursed with her mother's love of fatty foods. The good news is that God has provided tools for breaking the negative impacts of ancestral behavior. The negative impacts can and will be abated when we use these tools the way God instructs us. Remember, too, that God never forces us to be free from our issues. He offers us freedom if we are willing to take the necessary actions.

So how do generational curses manifest in our lives? How do we know when we are dealing with a generational curse rather than just a bad habit? How do we know what curses look like so that we can use God's tools properly?

Examples of Generational Curses:

LONGTIME FAMILY DISEASES:

Your grandmother had diabetes, your mother had diabetes, and now you either have or are expected to develop diabetes. The same goes for heart problems and other medical conditions that are based on poor health habits. Your ancestors may have eaten poorly or failed to take proper care of their physical bodies, but you can make the decision to change this and break this curse in your family today. You and your children and their children do not ever need to experience dialysis, kidney failure and glucose testing. Changes you make today can and will free your children from a life of hospital visits and bills.

MENTAL AND EMOTIONAL PROBLEMS:

The painful fact is that many people overeat or eat poorly because of other issues in their lives. Stresses at work and in people's lives, along with an inability to handle them contribute to many modern health issues. Wanting what you can't or don't have or fearing that you are less than or that your child will be deprived if you don't have certain material possessions, etc., can lead to a life of "chasing The Joneses" that can leave you stressed out no matter how much you have. It can also leave you so empty inside you can't help but stuff yourself with food.

SHOPPING, OVEREATING AND SEX AND WORK ADDICTIONS:

How many people do you know whose homes are filled with accumulated clutter—mail ordered boxes, gadgets, clothes… some barely used items? Most people would understand that such accumulation is a sign of something going on in the person's life that needs to be addressed. Likewise, accumulating excess fat by eating far more than one needs is a sign that something is wrong that needs to be addressed.

Part of the modern problem is that our food has been genetically altered to not only taste better, but to provide more nutrition and calories. Much of the results of this genetic tampering is still unknown, but is suspected to be negative. It is very difficult to eat well. Modern farming uses chemicals to kill pests, but what do those chemicals do to us? In addition, busy lifestyles, such as those that come with keeping up with the Joneses, can mean little time for cooking our own foods. Instead, we rely on fast factory processed foods and fast food, often deep fried or prepared with excessive amounts of butter, salt and sugar—all of which leads to hundreds of extra calories even in tiny portions—let alone the huge portions we usually eat.

Many documentaries have recently come out that show that Americans are suffering from an obesity epidemic that is the direct result of our overindulgence and over-reliance on fast food. Children as young as five and six years old are developing type two diabetes, which was once called "adult onset diabetes" because only adults got it after years and years of eating poorly. The children are suffering because their parents no longer have time to prepare proper meals. Families all over the country are struggling with this crisis.

Add to this the fact that in many poorer communities it is cheaper to buy a hamburger at McDonald's than a head of lettuce at a grocery store. In fact, many poor communities are called "food deserts" because of the lack of availability of fresh vegetables and whole foods.

But what's behind all of this? For many it's convenience and cheapness. Try finding a healthy fast meal; it's very hard. But unhealthy fast meals abound. But why do we have to eat fast? In most cases our lifestyle is dictated my by our values. If we value a new car, a new house, PlayStations, Xboxes, new cell phones and all the other trappings of materialism, we likely don't have much time, because we're so busy working. We've prioritized things and things don't care if we're healthy or not. For all the love we have for things, they have absolutely no love for us.

What does God think about this situation that's destroying American families? Hebrews 13:5 says, "Don't love money; be satisfied with what you have. For God has said, 'I will never leave you nor abandon you."

Most Americans are so busy chasing after money and the things that money buys, that they ignore God's word and suffer the consequences in their bodies and lives. This is what I mean by recognizing curse in your life and the world. Sometimes all that's required to find curse in our lives is to follow the crowd—just do what everyone else does. Although we may well do these things in ignorance, we still pay the consequences of disobedience and ignoring God's advice for our lives.

Do we really need such a big house or apartment? Do we really need the new car, the new clothes, the new product, the thing on TV that we've lived without all these years. Think about how important your cell phone is to you. Now that data plans are required on all phones, it's nearly impossible to have a cell phone for less than $50/mo. per phone. If you're single and only have one phone, that might be fine. However, if you have a family, you likely now see more than $200/mo. just for cell phones. Never mind that merely 10-20 years ago, no one knew what a cell phone was. If you're like most Americans, you also pay for another thing that used to be free—TV. In many areas of the country, including big cities, you can't even get reception unless you pay for cable or satellite TV. For many, that's another $200/mo. Speaking of things that used to be free, how much do you now spend on water? I wonder how long it will be before we have to pay for clean air to breathe. The price of homes has gone through the roof. They've also gotten much bigger for no good reason—families have gotten smaller. Many people find their home has rooms in it they don't even use except one or two times a year. And for all these extras, we need more money, more money, more money.

So we love money. We love making money, watching people win money, spending money—everything but saving money. People have less savings now than ever before. We have less savings and more debt than any generation before us. So much debt that most of us will never pay it off—not in this life anyway. We are living far beyond our means because of credit cards, loans and deferred payments. We can't afford the stuff we buy with cash, so we charge it.

We LOVE money. And we suffer a curse because of it.

If our children are fat and unhealthy, they will likely produce fatter more unhealthy children after them. Many people have no time for their families so they turn to the internet, to pornography, to television and the twisted values of Hollywood that leave them hating themselves, wanting plastic surgery (more money), wanting to be rock stars, movie stars and athletes instead of people who contribute value to society.

Because we love money, our politicians are corrupted and only work for those who give them money. They neglect the poor and the common man. They ignore the needs of education, the environment, healthcare, justice, peace, and quality of life issues like clean water.

Because we love money we are cursed with crime. People are killed for cars, sneakers, or jewelry. Drug dealers sell poison to make money. Addicts then steal and rob to get money for their habit. Alarms on cars. Alarms on homes. In many areas, people live behind bars in their own homes. Because we love money, some sons commit crimes and spend their lives in prison. Prisons eat up tax dollars and keep needed money from going to education, healthcare and other needed services. In some countries, people are still enslaved because of the love of money. Children are kidnapped and sold into slavery to work at sweatshops so companies can make just a penny more in profit on rugs, underwear, sneakers, and shirts. In the poor country of Bangladesh, children as young as three and four are even sold into slavery by their parents for as little as $3US to be used as camel jockeys in Saudi Arabia, where they have no rights, no power, no anything. And because we love money, we close our eyes to all of it.

Because we love money, we pay outrageous amounts for basic healthcare. Hospitals won't treat patients until they prove they can pay for it. Because we love money, people die who could be treated and live. In fact, President Obama said that the driving passion behind his healthcare law was his mother's inability to afford needed cancer surgery that could have saved her life. He said his worst memories were of her on her deathbed arguing with insurance companies to cover her treatments. Meanwhile, because we love money, surgeons charge $50,000-$100,000 to do an operation. College costs nearly $150,000 to $260,000 to complete just four years—much of which our children take on as debt that burdens them the rest of their lives. A mere two generations ago, it only cost $6,000 to go all the way through medical school. This is the curse of greed, which is the love of money.

Because we love money, many pastors fleece their flock instead of feeding it. The spiritual vacuum left in people's lives even pushes them further along this path of disobedience and curse. Rather than teaching people, they promote the values of the world and addict their followers to church entertainment masquerading as teaching and wisdom.

The love of money (aka, the sin of covetousness) is so prevalent in our country that a whole myriad of curses can be linked back to it including: Repeated mental and emotional problems; abuses of drugs and/or alcohol; shopping, overeating, sex and work addictions; uncontrollable anger; and depression. But, we don't have to live under this curse. We don't have to love money. We don't have to subject ourselves to the world's standards and create all this pain and suffering in our lives.

All of this is the result of a curse from which God wants us to be free. But regardless of God's desire, people all over the country, including many Christians, suffer from the curses that come from loving money.

Do you see now, sister, how important it is to recognize generational curse in our lives? So many issues can spring unknowingly from our daily behaviors, which we may not even realize are a direct result of violating God's principles and wisdom.

Because the love of money runs so deeply in our society it affects so many areas both directly and indirectly. I already mentioned a number of other curses that can stem from the love of money, but I want to come back to them now, because they may also come from other areas of people's lives.

MENTAL AND EMOTIONAL PROBLEMS: (FEAR RELATED)

In addition to originating in our quest for money and security, mental and emotional problems stem from dozens of places. One such place reveals itself in the pattern of abuses we've suffered as children that may also be intergenerational issues that our parents suffered. For example, it is not unusual for a parent with poor self-esteem to raise a child that is timid and also lacks self-esteem. After all, it is very hard to give your child something you do not have yourself. Il-prepared parents can be verbally and mentally abusive to their children with or without knowing it.

A great and horrible example of what I mean here is the movie *Precious*. In the film, an overweight young girl named Precious struggles under abuses of overbearing, unloving, drug-addicted mother. The film is hard to watch as the mother constantly berates her daughter. In one climactic scene, Precious' mother, played by Monique breaks down in front of the social worker when she finally admits to abusing Precious. She tells the social worker that she did what she did because she didn't know better—that no one ever loved her and no one ever treated her kindly. All of her life, Precious' mother was trying to heal from her own abuses while abusing her daughter and allowing the man she lived with to abuse her as well.

Unless it is stopped and broken, the pain, abuse and mental damage passes from abused mother to abused daughter or son and from abused father to abused son, daughter, wife or girlfriend.

Given the fairly recent history of enslavement for Africans in the Americas, it is a testimony to God's grace and our people's amazing resilient spirits that we aren't all abusive people trying to heal from our own abuse. The fact is, however, that Africans in the Americas and throughout the world have a profound power in our relationship with God that allows us to find healing to stop the chain of mental and emotional abuse.

ABUSES OF DRUGS AND ALCOHOL: (POWER RELATED)

It is not by accident that the 12-Step Program, which has proven to be the most effective program in history at helping addicts overcome addictions of all types, begins with belief in God and submission of one's will to him. When drugs have hold of the human mind and body, the fight against it can break down all personal resolve. Even people who refuse to believe in God turn to a "higher power" to help them stop themselves from self-destruction.

The intergenerational effects of having alcoholic or drug-addicted parents has been understood for so long that groups such as Adult Children of Alcoholics (ACA) and Al-Anon have been offering help for years. So impactful are the effects of being the child of an alcohol or drug addicted parent that the characteristics of such children have been studied for years and are even defined clearly in psychological literature. Dr. Janet G Woititz, in her book

Adult Children of Alcoholics has defined these 13 commonly identifiable traits that many children of alcoholics share:

1. Adult children of alcoholics guess at what normal behavior is.
2. Adult children of alcoholics have difficulty following a project through from beginning to end.
3. Adult children of alcoholics lie when it would be just as easy to tell the truth.
4. Adult children of alcoholics judge themselves without mercy.
5. Adult children of alcoholics have difficulty having fun.
6. Adult children of alcoholics take themselves very seriously.
7. Adult children of alcoholics have difficulty with intimate relationships.
8. Adult children of alcoholics overreact to changes over which they have no control.
9. Adult children of alcoholics constantly seek approval and affirmation.
10. Adult children of alcoholics usually feel that they are different from other people.
11. Adult children of alcoholics are super responsible or super irresponsible.
12. Adult children of alcoholics are extremely loyal, even in the face of evidence that the loyalty is undeserved.
13. Adult children of alcoholics are impulsive. They tend to lock themselves into a course of action without

giving serious consideration to alternative behaviors or possible consequences. This impulsively leads to confusion, self-loathing and loss of control over their environment. In addition, they spend an excessive amount of energy cleaning up the mess.

No stronger argument can be made for the evidence of generational curse than to have actual, definable characteristics that are shared across the human spectrum by people who have experienced the same phenomenon. Perhaps you recognize yourself in some of the characteristics above and realize that you have others who think and feel exactly like you because they too have endured the frustrations, pain, and struggle of being a child of an alcoholic parent. If so, Al-Anon and ACA are excellent groups that can help you find healing to break free from this generational curse.

UNCONTROLLABLE ANGER: (POWER RELATED)

For many people, it's not the abuse that they have endured that identifies their lives, it's the abuse they inflict on others through uncontrollable anger. There are many different reasons that one might suffer with uncontrollable anger including having a sense of powerlessness due to unmet needs, having poor coping skills or having a hormonal imbalance among others. For many others, they are simply modeling the behavior they saw in a parent. Although many times people who are abused become abusers, it's not always the case. Still, if you've had parents model uncontrollable anger to you, if faced with a similar situation, you may find yourself modeling it to the world. If you find your knuckles scarred from punching walls or your walls and property damaged from your tantrums and fits, you may be experiencing uncontrollable anger—also known as Anger Disorder or Intermittent Explosive Disorder.

As believers, one of the most transformational beliefs about God is that he is all-powerful. The idea that you are loved by an all-powerful God and that He wants you to be at peace trusting in his power, wisdom and guidance can break through a lot of personal anger and frustration.

DEPRESSION: (VICTIM/POWER RELATED)

Like uncontrollable anger, depression generally feels like uncontrollable melancholy. In fact, some people suffering from uncontrollable anger are actually depressed. In one sense, anger disorder turns those emotions on the outside world, but depression turns them inside.

Depression can also be caused by hormonal imbalances which can be treated with medicine, but sometimes depression is a signal that your mind is not focused right. Moreover, depression can also be an intergenerational or trans-generational problem passed down from parent to child. Here are some common symptoms of people with depression:

- Persistent sad or "empty" mood.

- Feeling hopeless, helpless, worthless, pessimistic and/or guilty.
- Substance abuse.
- Fatigue or loss of interest in ordinary activities, including sex.
- Disturbances in eating and sleeping patterns.
- Irritability, increased crying, anxiety or panic attacks.
- Difficulty concentrating, remembering or making decisions.
- Thoughts of suicide; suicide plans or attempts.
- Persistent physical symptoms or pains that do not respond to treatment.

If you see yourself in the list above, my sister, you may well be dealing with depression. I don't want you to feel that depression is a sign of any kind of spiritual weakness. Many times, depression is very similar to near or farsightedness. If you need to wear glasses or contact lenses because your eyes don't focus clearly, it doesn't mean anything is wrong with you. In the same way that the muscles or ocular nerves of your eyes can have trouble, so too can other parts of your body. There's no shame in that. For some people, the glands of their body simply do not produce enough serotonin or dopamine—the chemical neurotransmitters and hormones in your brain and body that regulate your emotions and make you feel happy or at peace and calm. Some people are able to manage this with the type of meditation and prayer that I talk about in this book. For others, medicine works better than meditation, because it helps replace those missing hormones without requiring the concentration or focus of meditation.

If you find that the practice of focusing your mind on scriptures doesn't seem to work for you, by all means seek help from your medical doctor. Attempting to apply Biblical scriptures to your life when your body is not producing the right chemical balances is not unlike having bad eyes and trying to read your Bible. Even though Jesus healed the blind, believers everywhere use glasses and contacts to see the word of God. He gave man the ability to create glasses and contacts just like he gave the ability to restore hormonal and neurotransmitter imbalances. There are many believers sitting in churches who use medication to help their bodies function property. If you need it, don't ever be ashamed or afraid to ask for it or to use it. You may even find you only need it long enough to help you get out of a rut long enough to care about focusing your mind on God's word.

POOR RELATIONSHIPS/MARRIAGES: (TRUST/ LOVE/FORGIVENESS RELATED)

Many of us suffer from an inability to trust, love, forgive or accept love that has its roots in intergenerational issues. One of the truest realities is that it is difficult for us to form a loving relationship when we have never seen one modeled to us. It is the young man raised without a father that has trouble loving a wife or girlfriend. And it is the daughter raised without the father in the home that has trouble understanding how a man should love her and how she should love a man.

The number of broken marriages in our society most frighteningly forecasts the coming number of broken marriages to come in the future of our society. People today dispose of relationships like they throw out old clothes or trade in old cars. The damage done by these less than committed bonds manifest problems in people's lives for years to come. Because of growing up in a broken home, many people don't feel safe in their relationships, don't trust their spouses, don't know how to give love or how to accept love. Many have no idea that couples fight and argue, but work things out. Some dread confrontation because they see it as a sign of the end.

God, of course, calls us to much more stable relationships that most people experience in the world today. God wants us to know how to love so that we not only have and experience loving relationships, but so that our children experience loving, caring and protective homes. He also wants us to have loving relationships because he wants us to be a demonstration of his love to the world. When we as believers fail to practice forgiveness and love in our lives, we miss the whole point of the story of Jesus. Paul said it best in 1 Corinthians 13: 1-3:

> *"If I speak in the tongues of men or of angels, but do not have love, I am only a resounding gong or a clanging cymbal. ² If I have the gift of prophecy and can fathom all mysteries and all knowledge, and if I have a faith that can move mountains, but do not have love, I am nothing. ³ If I give all I possess to*

*the poor and give over my body to hardship that I may boast,
but do not have love, I gain nothing."*

God wants us to know loving relationships because the whole
mission of Jesus on earth was a loving relationship. If you come
from a broken home or have failed in love in the past, you don't
have to give up on love or on your ability to know and experience
a secure loving relationship.

ANXIETY

Feeling worried about things in this world is something many
people face. The world can be a very scary place. I don't need
to outline all the ways in which things can go wrong for you to
understand and appreciate that there are plenty of reasons for
people to be anxious. Many times this sense of anxiety can pass
from parent to child both through epigenetic markers and through
conversations or passive interaction.

The mother who worries aloud about her health or the
father who complains about the poor condition of the world after
watching the evening news, can both, inadvertently, fill the child
with anxiety. This falls on top of the anxiety of childhood—the
bully at school, the final exam, the college admission, the job quest,
the "will I make it in the world?" fears that face all young people.

At times, it seems that society's main goal is to stress us out
and make us anxious. If it's not what's happening in the Middle
East, then it's what's happening on the city streets. If it's not the

economy, it's the pollution. If it's not the stuff they put in the food, it's the lack of food in other countries. If it's not technology taking over our lives, it's whether the next budget will take away our Social Security. There are so many things to care about and so many things to potentially be anxious about. But, as I mentioned earlier, God does not want us to be anxious about any of them. I'm not saying he does not want us involved and working to solve issues in our world—far from it. He wants us very present in bringing solutions to people. He just does not want to be anxious as we do it. He wants us to work at issues with the full peace that He is ultimately in control.

These issues and many more often find their ways through the very cells of our bodies transmuted from adult to child over generations. Many people have lived their entire lives in misery believing this is just how things are supposed to be—completely unaware that they could be living a more fulfilling, happier and more peaceful life.

In the Bible, David is an example of a person who creates a generational curse through his behavior that then passed down to his sons. Discontented with his many wives, David seduced Bathsheba, the wife of one of his soldiers. She becomes pregnant from the encounter. David then sends for Uriah to return from the battlefield for a time of leave hoping that he would have sex with his wife so that he will believe the baby is his. But Uriah is so faithful to David and Israel that he refuses to enjoy himself with his wife until his fellow fighters are also returned home. Because David's plan failed, David then sent Uriah back to the battlefield

and gave instructions to his General to place Uriah at the front
of the battle and then withdraw the army so that Uriah would
be standing alone. The plot worked and Uriah was killed. David
then took Bathsheba as his wife. The curse that came upon him is
recorded in 2 Samuel 12:9-12:

*Wherefore hast thou despised the commandment of the
Lord, to do evil in his sight? Thou has killed Uriah the Hittite
with the sword, and hastaken his wife to be thy wife, and has
slain him with the sword of the children Ammon.*

*Now therefore the sword shall never depart from thine
house; because thou hast despised me and hast taken the wife
of Uriah the Hittite to be thy wife.*

*Thus saith the Lord, Behold, I will raise up evil against
thee out of thine own house, and I will take thy wives before
thine eyes, and give them unto thy neighbor, and he shall lie
with thy wives in the sight of this sun.*

*For thou didst it secretly: but I will do this thing before
all Israel, and before the sun.*

And so it was. After King David committed adultery with
Bathsheba and murdered her husband, a curse was unleashed on
his family. His son Amnon raped his half-sister – Tamar; and
her brother Absalom murdered Amnon. A curse was released on
David's family such that it became dysfunctional. We see in 2
Samuel 15 that Absalom conspired to take away the throne from
his father and, in the process, slept with all of David's wives right

on the roof of the palace. What David originated through his disobedience to God, came back as a curse on him and his children.

In my personal life, I learned that I had a curse of strife. It never seemed to take long before any relationship I started turn sour. I often found myself without friends and wondering why. My relationships with girlfriends would often end suddenly over some unspoken offense. For many years, I said to myself that I did not care if someone stopped speaking to me. If they stopped talking, I'd stop talking. But on my first mission trip to Ethiopia in 2000, God allowed me to identify the curse so that I could get rid of it.

I traveled to Ethiopia with a dear friend and prayer partner Hyacinth. We were roommates and did everything together. Whenever you saw her, you would see me and vice-versa. In fact, most of the people on the trip thought she was my older sister. Being older, Hyacinth struggled a bit with walking and often required my help on steep, stony roads and paths. On the last day of the trip, we took a tour of the Ethiopian capital city Addis Ababa. We drove around the city all morning and did not return to the hotel until after mid-day. Nature had been calling for hours, but we were stuck on the bus. When we arrived at the hotel, I made a mad dash for the restroom and left Hyacinth behind. Because I was so focused on the urgency relieving myself, I neglected to tell her where I was going or why.

Because I had the key to the room, after I used the restroom, I returned to the hotel lobby to meet Hyacinth. She was visibly upset. She said to me, "Just because you didn't want to help me off the bus doesn't mean you had to run away and leave me." I explained my reason for leaving suddenly, but she refused to believe me. I thought it was a silly thing until Hyacinth cancelled a visit to an AIDS clinic we had planned together. I was baffled. She refused to speak to me for the rest of the day.

That evening, I had to find out why she was so upset. After dinner, we went back to the room and discussed the situation. I listened to her point of view, but it seemed impossible that she would be that upset by what I'd done. I began to worry that anything I said might offend her more. I decided to pray before giving any reply. I went to sleep and woke up early in the morning and began reading the Bible. As God would have it, I read 1 Peter 2:8-10. The passage speaks of Jesus as the cornerstone that people stumble over, because they refuse to believe his message when they find it offensive. I thought about how I offended my friend and felt convicted to make sure it was resolved.

The next morning, I walked through the events of the entire previous day with Hyacinth. When we got to the part where I left to go to the restroom, she mentioned that one of the ladies on the bus had commented that I did not want to help her anymore. The comment was completely false, but it was at the core of Hyacinth's pain. I reminded her that I had said no such thing and that it was said out of maliciousness. The woman did not know me or Hyacinth and there was no reason in the world that I would confide something in her rather than my dear friend. Once Hyacinth understood this, we were able to heal our friendship. Normally, I would have dismissed my friend's pain as being the result of her personal issues. If Hyacinth had not talked to me, I would have dismissed her as well and departed Ethiopia with the same number of friends with which I'd arrived, but this time was different.

It occurred to me later that these types of misunderstandings had plagued me my whole life. Then I realized it was not just me, but they had also plagued my mother. In the past, I think I may have always chalked it up to my being an immigrant and unfamiliar with American ways. I might have assumed that people had a problem with my accent or my culture or the way I dress. Either way, if people didn't talk to me, I would just pretend that I did not care and stop talking to them. *After all, I do not have to talk to anyone who does not want to talk to me,* I would tell myself, *I don't need them.* That left a long line of shattered relationships in my wake. Looking back, I see my mother had the same trait of not resolving issues and allowing them to destroy relationships—especially inside the family. She would do things that would alienate family members and then be upset that people were offended. I recognized similar traits in myself.

I also noticed the same traits appearing in my daughter. Believe me, my sister; few things are harder than getting two choleric personalities with self-protective and dismissive tendencies to get along. When my daughter became a teenager, she seemed to turn from a sweet, gentle person into a total stranger. Many a day, I cried out in my West Indian accent, "Lard Geesus, help me ya today!" She seemed confused about who was the adult and who was the child in the relationship. If she asked to go somewhere and I refused her permission, she wouldn't mouth off, but she would look deeply hurt and stop talking to me. I had to admit, watching her was watching myself as a teen. The only difference was that I could never let my mother see it or I'd get slapped across my face.

When she would have a falling out with her friends and I would notice she was upset and ask her what was wrong, she would say, "I don't want to talk about it." Soon she would make a remark like, "I don't care if such and such is my friend or not." It was the same cold, dismissive and self-protective attitude my mother and I both had. The curse that was in my mother's life and mine was passing to my daughter, so it became very important to me to break it.

I learned to get in touch with my own feelings when offenses arise. It became important for me to search my heart to see if I had done something to cause offense or to cause a person to have a bad attitude towards me. And sure enough, there were things I did. In Hyacinth's case, I could have told her that I had to use the restroom and would be right back prior to leaving, but I didn't. I didn't think of my traveling companion and how she would feel—I was completely focused on myself. When I returned, I could have taken time immediately to understand why she was upset and put a little more effort into apologizing or admitting my insensitivity, but I didn't. Instead, I dismissed her feelings as silly and went on about my business. I was insensitive and I've learned to be more sensitive.

Learning to be more sensitive, paying closer attention to my behaviors, and teaching them to my daughter helped to transform our relationship as well. For my daughter, I had to learn to put myself in her shoes and see the situation from her perspective in order to be more sensitive to her. In addition, I had to let her know that in order for things to work out between her and her friends, she had to let her friends know how their actions were affecting her instead of just cutting off the relationship. It was not honest nor godly to hide her feelings or to be passive-aggressive by acting cold and dismissive. To have healthy friendships, people must be honest, vulnerable and compassionate.

My situation may not seem drastic, but when your emotional life is under bondage it is hard to reach your potential in life. I thank God for revealing this curse in my life and helping me to break it, because if it was not broken, I would not have any space in my life for the work I do in overseas missions. For most of my life, I was so consumed with things that happened to me that I felt tormented. Unresolved issues led to my anger and self-focus and made me look at life through dark glasses. The first chance I got to bring up a wrong that was done to me, I took it and turned good things into bad.

As Christians, when we allow Christ to identify these curses in our lives and free us from them, we are able to move forward to our best lives. It might take some time, depending on the level of our faith, but it can be done. Generational curses do not need to control your life or the lives of your loved ones any longer. Now that we know what it looks like, sister, let's get to work on breaking these curses and moving these issues out of our lives.

Here are a few questions to help you identify generational curses in your own life. Please write the answers to these questions on a separate piece of paper or on a page in your computer:

1. This chapter referenced various types of "curses" that affect people. Based on the information presented, can you identify anything that might be a curse in your life, which you want to remove?

2. Do you see any behaviors in yourself that you also notice in one of your parents/grandparents/siblings that you do not like?

3. Are there any behaviors you do that could be classified as bad habits that you want to break because they are hindering you by stealing your time, energy, money, joy or other valuable resource?

4. Does your family suffer from any long-time or intergenerational diseases?

5. Nearly everyone in America struggles with issues related to money or the love of money. Do you see any ways in which the love of money is an issue for you and or your family? For instance: Is your spending under control? Do you live within your means or do you only make it because of credit cards and other debt?

6. Does anyone in your family suffer from drug or alcohol addictions?

7. Do you, like David, live under the guilt of some past sin that you feel you pay for over and over again?

8. Have you ever tried to make positive changes in your life and failed more than once in the same area?

9. Do you see any traits in your children that you recognize in yourself that you wish they did not have?

Working through these questions, using the list and the tree can help you identify possible generational curses that you can focus on removing throughout the rest of this book. Whether the issues you deal with rise to the level of a generational curse or not, the ideas and principles in this book can help you navigate your way to healing, growth and freedom.

Here is a prayer I recommend for you as you begin to identify generational curses you would like to break in your life:

Lord God, I come to you in the name of your son, Jesus Christ, seeking help and guidance as I begin to identify and get free from generational curses that have plagued my family for years. I know that you want the curse to stop with me, so I submit my will to yours. Please open my eyes to any and all issues that may have hindered me or my family members. Where I lack the will or strength, give me the will and strength to confront these issues and overcome them. Break all curses in my life through this process of fellowship, discovery and study. Give me the wisdom and courage to see not only the negative impact of my past actions, but the power and freedom available to me in following your path. Thank you for leading me on this path of growth and empowerment. In Jesus' name. Amen.

Mentally Related	Physically Related
Alcohol abuse	Cancer
Alcohol dependence	heart disease
Attention deficit disorder	high blood pressure
Attention deficit hyperactivity disorder	arthritis
Autism	blood disorders
Asperger syndrome	diabetes
Bipolar disorder	
Cocaine dependence	
Cognitive disorder	
Communication disorder	
Depressive disorder	
Developmental coordination disorder	
Dyslexia	
Dementia	
Epilepsy	
Schizophrenia	
Schizophreniform disorder	
Severe mental retardation	

Spiritually Related	Emotionally Related
Occult involvement	Anxiety
Practice witchcraft	Fear
Covenant breakers	possessiveness
False religion worshipping of idols	Verbal abuse
Worshipping of animals	Hatred
Worshipping object in creation	Drug abuse
	Rebellion
	Stealing
	Critical spirit

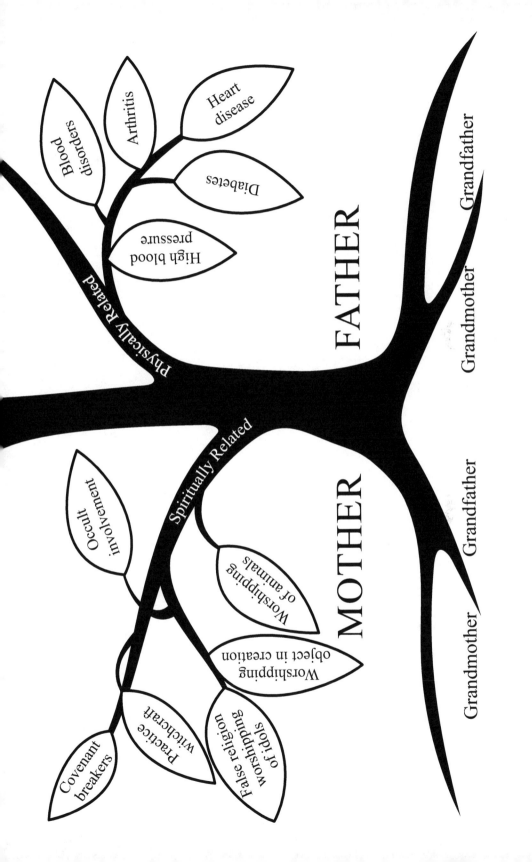

Chapter 5

BREAKING GENERATIONAL CURSES

"I can do all things through [Christ], who
gives me strength." ~Philippians 4:13

T
he process of breaking generational curses begins, as all types of healing should, with recognizing that a problem exists. Until we recognize that there is a problem in our lives, we cannot begin the processes necessary to find wholeness.

In the previous chapter, we discussed some ways in which generational curses may be manifesting in your life. In this chapter, we will look at breaking those curses and finding our way to a better, stronger, healthier and more fulfilling life.

When the children of Israel were about to take over the land of Canaan, God gave them a series of laws to obey in order to make sure they got the most benefit from the land—such as allowing the ground to lay fallow once every seven years so that it might rest and replenish itself. In addition, he gave a them a number of laws and rules designed to help them to stay mindful of God so that they would be a good society and not fall victim to selfishness, greed and other vices that would ultimately turn them against each other and the people surrounding them and leave them in a state of perpetual war. Almost immediately after taking over the land of the Canaanites, the Israelites began to ignore God's laws and do whatever they felt was right their own eyes. As a result, they offended both God and man, and found themselves being rebuked by God and threatened with exile in foreign lands as well as famine and war in their own.

In Leviticus 26:39-42, prior to their taking over the land, God told his people that they would have to pay for both their own sins and the sins of their ancestors if they ignored the laws he was giving them.

> *Those of you who survive will waste away in your enemies' lands because of their sins **and the sins of their ancestors**. But if at last my people will confess their sins **and the sins of their ancestors** for betraying me and being hostile toward me, which made me hostile toward them so that I sent them into the land of their enemies--then when their [disobedient] hearts are humbled and they [repent] for their sin, I will remember my covenant with Jacob and my covenant with*

Isaac and my covenant with Abraham, and I will remember the land. (Lev 26:39-42)

A few years ago, I read an article in the newspaper about the atrocities in the African country of Sudan. I read how the people in the Sudan were slaughtering each other. The point of view of the article was that the current U.S. President Bush should do something to help the people of the Sudan. As I looked at the pictures of the bodies of the massacred, I became so overwhelmed that I burst out with an inconsolable cry—a groaning from deep within my spirit. I began to pray for my people everywhere. During my prayer, I envisioned my African people standing shoulder to shoulder next to each other without any space in between each other. They were a sea of people just standing there. They all were looking in the same direction. In my prayers, I asked the Lord, "Why do my people have to suffer so much? Why are the daughters of my people brutalized?" When I was done crying and praying, what came into my spirit was a revelation.

The people of Africa are historically a very gentle, intelligent, and wise people. We built the earliest civilizations of Khemet/ Egypt and spread the knowledge of astronomy, calculus, numerals and this very alphabet you're reading now to the world. We even ruled in Europe up until the time of Christopher Columbus. We are responsible for the foundations of all understandings in science, mathematics and biology. Over the course of the last several hundred years though, the African slave trade and the racial ignorance, divisiveness, white supremacy mythology and bigotry that rose up to justify profiting financially off the free labor of innocent people, has left a wake of generational destruction in Black communities around the world. As a result, many Black people in the world have lost their ability to value and love each other as we should. In many ways, some of us have taken on the views of the oppressor and no longer see ourselves as worthy of love, respect, goodwill, compassion and fairness. Instead, we see ourselves in the way that white oppressors have taught us to see ourselves, after years and years of racial injustice, bigoted laws, unfair treatment and negative media images—as lazy, undesirable, stupid, hurtful, hateful, underachieving, worthless and less-than. The images many of us hold in our own minds of each other, and even ourselves, are often far from positive. We have been conditioned systematically to hate ourselves.

Because of this conditioning, we have come to believe in, and some even subconsciously worship, the idols that have been placed before us—mythological idols of white beauty, power and supremacy. We, thus, despise ourselves—our natural hair, our lips, our full bodies, our dark skin and those who look like us. We turn our back on the beauty and value that God gave us when he created us and instead turn to worship something low and base that man created. This act of turning from the truth of God to a manmade myth of inferiority that agrees with the false teachings of a white supremacy mythology is no different than the idol worship the Israelites practiced. We, as a people, have exchanged the truth of God for a lie of man. That lie has led us to hate ourselves and each other.

What occurred to me, when I read about those Sudanese people in Africa killing each other in such brutal ways, is that they had no appreciation or respect for their value as human beings. They hated each other. They had no value of love of each other as worthy of life and worthy of respect. They saw each other as obstacles to their own individual goals of power, wealth, money and control over resources so that they could have the wealth (love of money, greed) and power they saw their oppressors had (envy).

Prior to the invasion of their oppressors, most African people viewed the natural resources much like Native Americans viewed the natural resources of the planet—as belonging freely to all. The land did not belong to anyone—it was ancient and was to be shared, as it provided for everyone in the country. Tribes and nations were basically extended families that worked together to both access resources and maximize them. But under oppression, individuals learned that they could gain favor with the oppressor by selling out their own. They learned to think like their oppressors and to exchange their values of community for individual power. The most ruthless became warlords and formed alliances with their oppressors to strip the country of resources in exchange for weapons to help maintain their individual power. Thus a select group became very rich and powerful, while the rest of the country was driven to utter poverty and despair.

Over time, some who were previously abused rose up and seized power and did to their oppressors what had been done to them. The cycle continued until hatreds built over generations. All that disrespect for the value of human life and the truth of God's teaching is the cause of much of the continued suffering in the nation of Sudan just as it was for the nation of Israel. Romans 1:18-25 says:

The wrath of God is being revealed from heaven against all the godlessness and wickedness of people, who suppress the truth by their wickedness, since what may be known about God is plain to them, because God has made it plain to them. For since the creation of the world God's invisible quali-ties—his eternal power and divine nature—have been clearly seen, being understood from what has been made, so that people are without excuse. For although they knew God, they neither glorified him as God nor gave thanks to him, but their thinking became futile and their foolish hearts were darkened. Although they claimed to be wise, they became fools and exchanged the glory of the immortal God for images made to look like a mortal human being and birds and animals and reptiles.

Therefore God gave them over in the sinful desires of their hearts.... They exchanged the truth about God for a lie, and worshiped and served created things rather than the Creator—who is forever praised. Amen.

The gospel of Jesus Christ was in Sudan and Ethiopia much earlier than it was in Europe. It was carried there by the Ethiopian Eunuch, who, if you recall from his conversion story in the book of Acts, was visiting Jerusalem to worship because he was a practicing Jew. These nations are very much aware of their sin against God. Have they been oppressed? Yes. Have they been abused, turned against each other and rewarded for evil, treason against their own people and murderous greed? Yes. Is it the oppressor's fault? Yes.

All of these things are true, but they, like we, are still accountable for their actions. God will punish those who have done the evil of turning our people against each other. That is his work of judgment to do. Our work is to obey the Lord. After all, just because someone else breaks the law and seems to get away with it, that fact does not give us any right to break the law. Nor does the fact that someone else breaks the law mean that we will not be held accountable if we break the law. We may not see how God is judging those who enslaved our people.

To many, it might seem as if nothing but prosperity has followed those nations that perpetrated such evil against an innocent people, but only God knows what he has in store. Romans 12:19 says, "Dear friends, never take revenge. Leave that to the righteous anger of God. For the Scriptures say, 'I will take revenge; I will pay them back,' says the LORD." Just as we are to never take revenge, we are to "do unto others as we *would have them do unto us.*" We can't do to them *what they do to us* or we will be just as guilty as them. As Martin Luther King Jr. said, quoting Mahatma Gandhi, "The philosophy of an eye for an eye leaves everyone blind." Our calling is to represent Christ. That may mean we suffer. However, in our suffering, we are still required to do right. God does not look the other way if we sin because we have been sinned against.

My sister, this truth is the key to understanding everything that I'm writing about in this book. There may be many good reasons for our behavior. Drug dealers say they have no other options, "If I don't sell it, someone else will. What else can I do with my criminal record?" Pimps and pushers say the same kinds of things. Sisters who sell their bodies say they are "doing what they have to do." Greedy corporate bankers, lawyers and lobbyists swear they, too, must do what they do to remain competitive. "Everyone is doing it." Yet each and every one of them, just as each and every one of us, is subject to the law of God and God's judgment. But what if they don't know? What if they have never heard the gospel? It doesn't matter because, as Paul said in the book of Romans above, God's law is obvious to all in nature. Men know they are doing wrong but they do not care and do wrong anyway. They "exchange the truth of God for a lie and worship and serve created things (money, fame, power, sex) rather than God.

The evidence that a self-hating curse has come upon our people is clearly seen in the majority of rap and music lyrics. Young black men and boys today use the N-Word to refer to each other more than the oppressors used it to belittle our dignity and enslave our minds and spirits. Words in songs refer to women— mothers, daughters, sisters, aunties—the life-givers and nurturers of our society as nothing more than sexual objects, female dogs and prostitutes. Rather than women being the recipients of love, protection, admiration and care, songs make them out to be unscrupulous manipulators, good for nothing more than taking off their clothes and satisfying a man's primal urges. Our young men, rather than being the protectors of our race, have become the scourge of our society—killing each other, killing innocent children, running rampant throughout our communities and making older people fear them for their lack of discipline, lack of focus, lack of manners, lack of direction and lack of respect. This curse came upon us when we turned from the Martin Luther King Juniors, Malcolm Xs and strong civil rights leaders of the '50s and '60s and began to follow instead the movie and TV actors portraying pimps and pushers on the big screens of the '70s. When we went from men like Medger Evers to pimps like Superfly and Huggy Bear, we began a downward spiral that left our young men dazed and confused by a value system at war with God's values.

Today, with the voices that once sang praises in churches and anthems of peace, freedom and hope, we sing the very lyrics that berate us, humiliate and denigrate our persons. Young black men drive down the streets blasting vulgar, misogynistic, racist and humiliating lyrics for the whole community to hear. Men and women, who walked with King for the right to live in good neighborhoods with good schools, get serenaded with songs a Klansman could only have dreamed of writing. One rap song by Schoolboy Q and Kendrick Lamar is so twisted that it uses the N-Word 39 times. And guess what the name of the song is? It's called, "Blessed." Yes, they have a song called "Blessed" that says the N-Word 39 times. What is blessed about being an n-word 39 times? Only a twisted, sick mind could imagine such a thing. Young women sing songs referring to themselves as the B-word. None of it is okay. Not at all.

But how do we change it? How do we turn around decades of damage or even hundreds of years of damage dating back to the days of our physical bondage? First, we begin by recognizing it exists and that it is not okay. That it is wrong. Wrong-minded and destructive. We must, in our society and in our personal lives, begin to identify the things that damage us and recognize where they come from and how we are allowing them into our lives. After all, Kendrick Lamar and Schoolboy Q didn't give themselves record contracts, right? Someone is paying them to destroy our communities. When we listen to their music, we are supporting those who wish to destroy us. There is an entire entertainment culture that thrives on destroying black people and promoting those who help destroy black people psychologically, emotionally, mentally and spiritually.

Imagine, if you can, any other artists out there of any other race who used racist slurs against their own people like black rappers use against their own people. Would they ever get a record contract—let alone be lauded by the industry and nominated for Grammys as Kendrick Lamar was? No. You can't think of a single artist other than Black artists, because no other people get paid to destroy and debase their race but ours. For some reason, paying black people to destroy other black people is perfectly fine.

Unfortunately, there always seems to be a line of weak-minded, sick, lost and self-hating black people oppressed, degenerate and willing enough to do anything for money. Just as there were self-hating black people who went into the countrysides of Africa as guides to help white enslavers trick and kidnap innocent black young men, women and children hundreds of years ago so they could profit from exploiting their people, so today that same spirit lives on. It lives in self-hating black folk working to enslave innocent children with lyrics spurring them to destructive lives. These lyrics promote: crime, worshipping money; worshipping clothing designers; worshipping liquor manufacturers; worshipping car manufacturers; all while perpetuating self-hatred, violence, debasement, immorality, and distrust of our own people.

How do we change this? After recognizing it, the second key is the same as it has always been—to repent before God. To restore God's values and God's truth to the throne of our lives. To exchange the values of the world that we have adopted and return to the values of God. To say no to the idols the world puts before us that make us act outside of God's will for purposes of our own glory, greed, power, ego, or advantage. Instead, we can offer ourselves as God's servants eager to help, love, encourage, give, share, uplift, motivate, strengthen, sacrifice, teach, improve and respect ourselves and each other.

You may be asking, "But how do I do this?" It's a good question, because this is not easy. I never said it would be easy. It is not easy to stand against a constant tide of negative, selfish imagery that tempts us towards disempowering behavior, satisfies our sinful natural cravings, or boosts our ego. But God is in the business of helping us do what we cannot do by ourselves. Philippians 4:13 says, "I can do all things through [Christ], who gives me strength." So this fight is not a fight you fight alone. It is a fight you fight alongside someone who has unlimited strength to supply you all the energy and power you need. You fight this fight with all the power of the Lord God himself. And as Paul says in Romans 8:31, "If God be for us, who can be against us?" The answer to that question is no one.

The Bible tells us that we are to love the Lord our God with all our heart, mind and strength and that we are to love our neighbors as we love ourselves. Jesus said these two commands summarize the entire Torah—all of the teaching of the Old Testament. But if we don't love ourselves, how can we love our neighbors? How can we love God? The key then is first learning to love ourselves. To love ourselves we must see ourselves as God sees us—as worthy, as lovely, as important, as unique, as gifted, as beautiful, as intelligent, and as fearfully and wonderfully made. We must realign our thinking about ourselves with what God says about us rather than what rap lyrics say about us. We must understand our position in life and our importance to the world as Jesus understands it and teaches it rather than as the news media reports it. We must begin to readjust our thinking about ourselves so that we see our worth based on what God's Word says, not what our bank account says, not what our clothing label says, not what the symbol on my our car says, and certainly not what Hollywood or the media says.

My sister, you are worthy of respect. You are worthy of love and you deserve love. You are beautiful. I don't have to see you to know you are beautiful, because beauty isn't about what you look like, it is about who you are. You are beautiful. You are lovely. You are fearfully and wonderfully made. You are awesome. You are blessed. You are gifted. You are a blessing to the world. You are one in a billion, billion. Think about it. Think about all the things that had to happen for you to exist in this world today—for you to be reading this sentence right now. Think of all the miracles and odds you beat. When you were conceived, you were the one cell of billions of cells that found the egg and fertilized it.

Have you ever thought about the miracle of your birth? If any of the other cells had reached the egg first, you would have never existed. Before you were even born, you were a CHAMPION. A winner. Lucky. Blessed. A SURVIVOR! You were Chosen. So don't you ever accept any treatment from any person that makes you feel less than you truly are. Never allow anyone to downplay or discount your contribution, your opinion, your value, your view, your intelligence or your worth. When you begin to see yourself as God sees you, you raise your expectations of the world and others. You begin to expect to be treated properly and you stop tolerating anything less than that.

You must cultivate this attitude in yourself if you are going to break generational curses in your life and your family's lives. Those who went before you that fell victims to these curses did so because they did not know who they were in God. When we lose our connection to God, we lose our identity, power and wisdom. When we restore our connection to God, we restore our vision and begin to see the world as God sees it. But more importantly, we begin to see ourselves as God sees us. We begin to see our family members as God sees them.

The word 'repent' means to change one's mind. To change your mind, you usually must have new information. When we repent, we are turning from our old view of the world and ourselves and going in the direction of the new information. The new information you are learning from God's word is intended to help you change your mind about how you view the world, your life, your family, your values, your worth, your power and your relationship to God. It is up to each of us to make the decisions necessary to reinforce this new behavior in our lives and to model it before our loved ones if we want to see them break free from generational curses.

PRAYER

Heavenly Father, I come before you in the name of my Lord and Savior Jesus Christ. I praise and thank you for the redemptive power of the blood of Jesus; **who has redeemed us from the power of the law.** I confess all sins that have given the enemy legal right to operate any curse on me and my household. Father, Jesus said in John 14, **if I ask any thing in His name You will do it.** So, Father I repent and ask You to forgive me for any ways, thoughts, deeds and actions that have brought me to this point in my life. Please remove and destroy all curses, word curses and generational curses coming from my sins, the prayers of others, or from my fore-parents. Lord, sever and destroy every evil thing with all their effect, side effects, stings, roots and tentacles. Lord, burn them at their roots so they cannot come back on me or my family again, in the name of Jesus and through the power of the Holy Spirit. Amen!

QUESTIONS FOR DISCUSSION

1. Do you sometimes feel like something is wrong in your life, but you cannot verbalize what is wrong?

2. What are these two Scriptures saying about Knowledge and truth: Hosea 4:6 and John 8:32 and 36?

3. What does James 5:16 say we must do in order to be healed?

4. Why do we want these curses to be broken off our lives?

5. What do you understand about yourself, your value and your relationship to God now that you did not understand before and how does that affect your view of yourself?

Chapter 6

DESTROYING STRONGHOLDS

*"We demolish arguments and every pretension that sets itself
up against the knowledge of God, and we take captive every
thought to make it obedient to Christ." 2 Corinthians 10:5*

Recently, the actress Lupita Nyong'o won the Academy Award for best actress for her portrayal of a slave in the movie 12 Years a Slave. In her acceptance speech, through tearing eyes, she told the world that she never believed it would be possible for someone like her to win, because she had always believed that her dark skin made her ugly and unwanted. Many Black women across the world felt her pain in that moment. Being a woman of dark hue myself, the statement hit me at the core of my being. It evoked a deep feeling of both pain for us and sympathy for my sister who had just exposed herself. Most of us, like her, had been told negative self-hating things or come to believe them, because of one reason or another and have carried them throughout our lives. Weeks later, Lupita's face appeared on the cover of the last place she expected to ever appear—People Magazine's Most Beautiful People in the World issue. Because of her belief, the truth of her beauty was hidden from her all of her life. In the same way, the truth of the beauty we possess can be hidden from us as well. That is the effect of strongholds.

Stronghold is a military term given to a walled city or a castle fortress to defend it from enemy attack. But when it comes to our own lives, strongholds are our subconscious mind operations that control our ways of thinking and acting. Psychologists and therapists refer to them as cognitive distortions. They are walls we erected to control our mind, which consist of our emotions, our will and our intellect—these elements of our human nature are also known as the "flesh." They appear as our normal perceptions and ways of being, because they were built when we were young children between the ages of 0 to 6 years old, so we hardly even remember when we begin to think in certain ways. These 'mind walls' protect our emotions in times of distress, anger, guilt, pain, unmet needs, hidden sin, bitterness, feelings of rejection, unfor-giveness and pride. But they also keep out the Knowledge of God, the truth about God and block the purpose and plan of God in our lives.

These mindsets are disobedient to the law of God, so Satan uses them to his advantage. Because they were developed before we accepted Jesus Christ as our personal Savior, they do not subject themselves to the law of God (Romans 8:7) and are not automatically destroyed when we come to faith. Because they are the product of our own mind, and not some outside force or being, they can't be cast out. In order to overcome strongholds, we must WORK at it. For many therapists dealing with people who have cognitive distortions or strongholds, the greatest frustration, and the point at which many clients quit therapy, is in doing the work to fix their distorted thinking.

Now that you have taken the steps of repentance and broken the generational curses, you must now learn to destroy strongholds in your life so that you can live in the fullness of victory and so that generational curses do not return because generational curses usually begin with strongholds. The strongholds we nurture and coddle or allow to continue in our lives give birth to generational curses down the line.

This chapter will explore the origin of strongholds in people's lives and how they work against the growth and power God wants us to experience. Together, sister, we will explore how most strongholds develop in people as children, because the child mind cannot properly understand or address some of the issues a young child might confront. As a result, attitudes and beliefs take root that war against the word of God and encourage destructive rather than constructive behaviors and habits.

Because these strongholds often develop at a young age, the tendency of people is to believe that they were born damaged or inferior and are, therefore, incapable of change. The behavior is so familiar that many can't even imagine their lives being lived any other way. Such attitudes discourage people from walking the paths God designed for them to walk. As a result, they lead defeated lives, which only goes to strengthen the stronghold and perpetuate the generational curse.

However, we must learn to destroy strongholds. In order to destroy strongholds, we must first identify them. In order to identify them, we must move towards the things we fear because doing so usually reveals where strongholds are hiding.

In this chapter, we're going to look at some people from the Bible and how they faced and overcame similar strongholds. Together, we will work through meditation and prayer to "loose"— shatter, destroy, remove, crush or break asunder—the strongholds that have deceived us our entire lives. To destroy strongholds, it is best that we follow a specific and proven process that includes the following 4 steps:

1. Repentance—gives authority to God to intervene in our lives and breaks Satan's power.

2. Binding thoughts, will and emotions to the truth and will of God. The power of strongholds is that they are made of emotions and will or "flesh," which the Bible says, "must be put to death on the cross." The process of binding relates to your developing a new way of thinking about life.

3. Prayer to loose/break all protective strongholds around the deception in place in your life.

4. Encouragement to endure the process. The change the
    you seek in this process is spiritual and requires time,
    patience, focus and will to complete.

In order for actress Lupita Nyong'o to overcome her stronghold, she had to face her fears. Years and years spent auditioning
for roles and facing rejection would seemingly reinforce her belief
about her looks, but whether she was conscious of it or not, she
was doing the work of breaking strongholds by constantly facing
the thing she feared. As an actress, she had to keep putting herself
in a position of being rejected if her dream of becoming an actress
would ever come to fruition. Little did she realize how much her
persistence would be rewarded. It was beyond her wildest dreams
to be on the cover of a magazine as one of the world's most beautiful people, but that is a perfect illustration of what God has in
store for us when we overcome our strongholds as well—a life
beyond our wildest dreams.

The Prophet Elijah in the Bible is another person who dealt
with strongholds in his life. When you think of mighty men of God,
few come to mind mightier than the prophet Elijah. Elijah had a
number of accomplishments in his life that certainly don't sound
like the characteristics of someone struggling with a stronghold,
but a closer examination reveals more than meets the eye. Elijah is
one of those people in the Bible that does not have an origin story.
When we meet Elijah in the book of 1 Kings 17:1, he is already a
prophet and already threatening King Ahab.

Elijah shows up in the Bible fully formed. We don't know where he was born. We don't know anything about his childhood. We don't know where he got his training, how he got his calling into ministry, or how he got an audience with the king. All we know is that he's from a town called Tishbe in Gilead. But from the time he is introduced, he is the main character of the story. He tells Ahab, *"As surely as the LORD, the God of Israel, lives—the God I serve—there will be no dew or rain during the next few years until I give the word!"* And with that he starts his epic feud with the King of Israel and his infamous wife Jezebel, who worshipped the idols Baal and Asherah instead of the Lord. In fact, it was Ahab's disobedience to God that lead Elijah to confront him.

What amazing confidence Elijah displayed. To confront a king who had the power of life and death over people and to make that announcement took confidence, right? Later, among his many adventures, he raises a boy from the dead. He is fed by ravens and travels in a whirlwind. After three years, he returns to King Ahab whose nation has begun to fall apart, and challenges his priests of Baal and Asherah to a test to show which God is true. Whichever prophet can call down fire from heaven is the true God and the prophets of the false god are to be put to death. Well, if you know the story, Elijah wins and orders all the prophets of Baal and Asherah to be brought to him so he could slay them by his own hand. When Ahab told Jezebel what happened, she sent a messenger to Elijah saying she was going to kill him. And look at what it says in 1 Kings 19:3, *"And he [Elijah] was afraid and arose and ran for his life and came to Beersheba, which belongs to Judah, and left his servant there."*

Here was a man who had killed 850 false prophets with his hands the day before. And now he was running for his life. But that's not all. He was so afraid that he ran to the desert and hid beneath a tree and asked God to kill him. The Bible says in 1 Kings 19 v. 5-9 that an angel came and ministered to him and fed him food. Still Elijah, the mighty prophet of God, was afraid and used the energy of that food to run away further—traveling forty days and nights until he came to the Mt. Horeb, where he hid in a cave. At that point, God himself showed up and asked him why he was there.

How can it be that a man as anointed, chosen, full of power and grace as Elijah could be so frightened by the threat of a woman he knew was wicked? The answer lies in strongholds. Just as Elijah's fear was irrational and impossible for us to understand, so is the power of stronghold in our lives.

Sometimes we find ourselves doing things we can't explain or even understand—irrational, stupid, weak and insane things that often turn our lives upside down. We fear for no good reason. We take silly comments personally. We are full of anger or rage at things that are out of our control. We drink ourselves into car accidents. We eat ourselves into obesity. We kick ourselves when we're down. We hate ourselves, judge ourselves, and judge others. We mouth off at the wrong people for the wrong reasons. We spend money on things we don't want. We go into debt for things to impress people we don't even like. We waste our time watching people act stupid on TV. We can't resist spreading gossip. We can't stop ourselves from saying something mean. We hit. We fight. We abuse. We make other people crazy so that they abuse. We worry about what other people think so much that we're afraid to be ourselves. We talk ourselves out of good things. We doubt our abilities. We doubt our intelligence. We doubt our chances of success. We give up before we start. We blame others. We blame ourselves. We blame our parents. We blame our children. We blame God. We fail to take responsibility. Or we take too much responsibility. We try to fix people. We interfere in other people's lives. We worry. We annoy. We complain, whine, and expect the worst to happen.

When a stronghold is present in our lives, irrational, distorted thinking is always present as well. If you find people asking you, "Why do you keep doing that?" They may be pointing at something irrational in your life. If your actions make no sense to people, or seem way out of proportion to the situation, you may want to look at whether there is a stronghold at work in your life.

But the best place to search out strongholds is in the same place where Elijah found his—hiding among his fears. Strongholds love to hide in the cave of our fears because it is the things we fear the most that we are most trying to guard against. It is the things we fear the most that build up the most walls to avoid.

If we fear rejection, look for a stronghold built around avoiding rejection. Perhaps you find yourself stuck in a dead-end job because you fear the rejection of applying for a new one, you doubt your abilities, or you think you are not smart enough.

Maybe you settle for being miserable in your work because you fear someone will fin out that you're looking for a job and fire you. Maybe you fear you will find out that you can't get another job. Whatever it is that you fear, your stronghold is a defense against the pain you anticipate will come to you.

As I said earlier, pain, in whatever form it takes, is central to controlling our behavior. Strongholds are nothing more than the walls we build in our minds that we believe, and usually falsely, will insulate us from pain.

When God asked Elijah why he was hiding in the cave on Mt. Horeb, Elijah said, *"I have zealously served the Lord God Almighty. But the people of Israel have broken their covenant with you, torn down your altars, and killed every one of your prophets. I am the only one left, and now they are trying to kill me, too."*

In response to Elijah's fear, God does something remarkable. 1 Kings 19:11 says that God gives Elijah a display of his power: *"Go out and stand before me on the mountain," the Lord told him. And as Elijah stood there, the Lord passed by, and a mighty wind-storm hit the mountain. It was such a terrible blast that the rocks were torn loose, but the Lord was not in the wind. After the wind there was an earthquake, but the Lord was not in the earthquake. ¹²And after the earthquake there was a fire, but the Lord was not in the fire. And after the fire there was the sound of a gentle whisper. ¹³When Elijah heard it, he wrapped his face in his cloak and went out and stood at the entrance of the cave.*

God was testing Elijah to see if he still recognized his voice. Did Elijah still understand that he was working for God Almighty or had he forgot? At the end of the test, Elijah proved he still recognized God's presence, but it didn't change anything for him. He was still afraid and went back and stood at the entrance of the cave covering his face with his cloak.

God asked him again, "What are you doing here, Elijah?" And Elijah replied in verse 14 exactly as his did before, *"He replied again, "I have zealously served the Lord God Almighty. But the people of Israel have broken their covenant with you, torn down your altars, and killed every one of your prophets. I am the only one left, and now they are trying to kill me, too."*

Here was a man who had an actual, physical audience with God and who still was so controlled by his stronghold that even in God's very presence, he refused to overcome it. Finally, God said in verse 15-16, *"Go back the same way you came, and travel to the wilderness of Damascus. When you arrive there, anoint Hazael to be king of Aram. ¹⁶Then anoint Jehu grandson of Nimshib to be king of Israel, and anoint Elisha son of Shaphat from the town of Abel-meholah to replace you as my prophet."*

Elijah's stronghold brought an end to his ministry. God was unable to continue to use him because of his irrational fear. Elijah refused to let go the cognitive distortions he held in his own mind even under the direct counsel of God. This shows us that God will not remove these distortions for us—we have to do the work ourselves. And it also shows us that it's not easy work to do.

Having strongholds present in our lives does not mean we won't be able to live our lives. It means we won't be able to live them as powerfully and fully as we could. Irrational thoughts and feelings, cognitive distortions of reality and other types of twisted thinking do not serve us in any positive way. Though it may seem that expecting the worst, putting yourself down, or being critical or doubtful is comforting, all these things really do is keep us from achieving our best in our lives.

WHY WE MUST DESTROY STRONGHOLDS

There are some Believers who keep having an Israelite experience—going around in the wilderness time after time—repeatedly floundering and struggling with the same problems, hang-ups, and fears that plagued them before they gave their lives to Jesus. Yet, there are others who made the same commitment to Christ, but they rise above their problems, hang-ups, and fears, and go on to live victorious and exciting Christian lives. What is the difference between the two?

The problem is that even after our spirit has been resurrected by the power of Jesus Christ, our hearts and minds are still bombarded with painful memories and experiences from our youth that affect our lives over time. When God's truth, God's promises, God's love, and God's will for His plan and purpose for our lives tries to penetrate, it is blocked by the strongholds we erected. As a result, we live in defeat. We struggle. We experience fear, anger, bitterness, unforgiveness, rejection and we exude pride. When this happens, we cannot be healed from the wounds we sustained before we came to Christ. In order to be healed, we must face our pain directly.

HOW DO WE DESTROY STRONGHOLDS?

Strongholds are erected and fortified around issues we are afraid to confront. You can tear down the wall that protects the grip of wrong patterns of thinking, wrong beliefs and wrong attitudes and be healed. We have to use the tool of binding and loosing in the name of Jesus to break that carnal mind. Take every one of our thoughts captive to the obedience of Jesus Christ (2 Cor. 10:5). Declare war on individual strongholds because they don't want to die. Firstly, we repent - ask God to forgive us for giving our mind the authority that is truly His. Repentance breaks Satan's power of control over you.

Bind your thoughts, your will, your emotions and life to the Truth and the Will of God in the name of Jesus Christ. Strongholds cannot be cast out because they are our emotions and will. Thus, they are our flesh and we have to put our flesh to death on the cross. Learn and meditate on the Word to gain strength. Build new ways of thinking. As actress Lupita Nyong'o forced herself to face the very rejection she feared all her life, she eventually broke through and overcame her stronghold that kept her from seeing her beauty. Likewise, by forcing ourselves to face the things we fear and "wage war against them" or "put them to death," they eventually lose their grip on our hearts and minds. When we challenge ourselves to try, to speak up, to dare, to risk, to stay disciplined, to endure, we find an eventual breakthrough against doubt, fear, regret, insecurity and failure. By affirming out position and power in Christ, we gain strength to take baby steps towards our healing.

Each time we push against the thing we fear, we find more success, more strength and more power to keep going. One step becomes two, which becomes walking, which becomes running and living a new life.

Pray to loose (to shatter, destroy, remove, crush or break asunder) all protective strongholds around the deception that was in place all your life. As you begin to do this, it will become uncomfortable, but you must stay with it. It is the strongholds fighting to stay in place.

Your prayer and meditation on God's word will help you develop new ways of thinking, new neural pathways and new thoughts.

When something as gentle as water drips on something as hard as a rock over time, the water will wear a groove in the rock. The greatest example of this is the Grand Canyon. But on a much smaller scale, constant dripping water will wear tiny fissures in the hardest stone, so that each time water hits the stone, it travels down the same path. This is how strongholds work. If we want the water to go in a different path, we must cut a new path in the stone though discipline and effort—otherwise, the water (thoughts, emotions) will continue to travel in the same negative and unwanted pathways. Taking action in the direction of our fears—challenging our flesh and declaring war on our old habits— cuts new paths in the stone so that the water (our thoughts, our feelings, our emotions) will flow in a positive, helpful direction.

PRAYER AGAINST STRONGHOLDS:

Lord Jesus, help me to identify the strongholds at work in my life and help me to break their bond on me so that I might live the best life I can and demonstrate your power and healing to all those around me. Help me to have the will and discipline to declare war and fight the good fight against old habits that have been with me as long as I remember. My desire is to live in victory and I know you desire that same goal. I declare victory over strongholds that have hindered me in the past and I break asunder their control over my life. In Jesus' name I pray. Amen.

My sister, I wish I could tell you that the battle against strongholds is a one-time fight. Unfortunately, that is not usually the case. Strongholds are called strongholds for a reason and must be continuously attacked and challenged until they are defeated once and for all. In the meantime, however, once you face them, they will weaken their grip on your life. If you challenge them consistently, they will break quicker. Stay strong in this battle and treat yourself with love and understanding as you do. There is no need to beat yourself up if you give into a stronghold—in fact, Satan is empowered and you are weakened if you begin to do Satan's job for him by accusing and condemning yourself. You are forgiven in Christ. His blood protects you and shields you from all condemnation. You are a child of God and beloved of God. God is on your side and he knows our weaknesses. He knows your heart and his is there to help encourage you. The only words you should be saying to yourself are words of love and encouragement. Words that build you up and reinforce your value in Christ. Don't give up. Fight the good fight and know that, in the end, you will win.

To help you stay strong in your battle against strongholds, let's talk more about the Blood of Jesus and the forgiveness that is yours through your faith. The next chapter will detail the ways in which you can release the covering blood of Jesus in your life on a daily basis so that Satan can no longer gain the mental and emotional stronghold in your life through guilt or self-condemnation.

CHAPTER 7

RELEASE THE BLOOD OF JESUS

"In fact, according to the law of Moses, nearly everything was purified with blood. For without the shedding of blood, there is no forgiveness." ~Hebrews 9:22

The role of blood in the Bible cannot be disputed. After the very first sin committed by Adam and Eve, God slayed the very first animal in order to provide a covering for their sin. From that point forward, God required his people to regularly offer sacrifices of animals and their blood in order to "make holy" both the people worshipping God and the items that were used to worship him.

What we did not know in the times of the Old Testament, was that God was foreshadowing the ultimate sacrifice his own son would make on the cross on behalf of humans. When animals shed their blood and gave their lives for our sins, our sins were forgiven for a time. However, these sacrifices had to be repeated regularly in order to maintain a right relationship with God. However, when Jesus shed his blood on the cross of Calvary, the fact that he is an eternal being meant that his blood was an eternal sacrifice, sufficient to cover the sins of all humankind forever. That is why it says in the New Testament in John 3:16, *"God so loved the world that he gave his only begotten son that whosoever believes in him shall not perish, but have everlasting life."* The everlasting life we gain by believing in Jesus Christ is because Jesus gave his life for us. Therefore, when God looks at the believer now, he sees his own son—forgiven, innocent, pure, holy and righteous. In the Old Testament, the blood of animals forgave us for a short time, but the blood of Jesus forgives us for eternity.

This is a marvelous truth, my sister, and one that you must hold onto in order to give you the strength and courage to continue to stand against the strongholds that may exist in your life.

As I mentioned in the previous chapter, one of Satan's strongest weapons is the accusations he makes against us to heap guilt on us for our shortcomings. We fall into a trap when we aid Satan by heaping more guilt on ourselves. When we condemn ourselves or shame ourselves and others, we are aiding Satan in destroying the morale, motivation and mentality of believers. Jesus warns us not to judge and he also says that we should love our neighbors as we love ourselves. If we are judging and condemning each other, we are not obeying Jesus. But the deeper secret that we often miss is that if we are judging and condemning ourselves, we also are not obeying Jesus.

Say that again, you ask? I will.

If we are judging and condemning ourselves, we also are not obeying Jesus. You should be shouting now if you understand what this means. This means there should never flow through your mind or lips another self-condemning thought that makes you feel less than or makes you think negatively of yourself in any way, shape or form. Why? Because Jesus Christ died to make you perfect before God. You are perfect, my sister, and you must come to understand that when you say otherwise, you are disagreeing with God. You may not feel perfect, but we are speaking in the spiritual sense. We are perfect in the spirit and it is our work as believers in Christ to get our minds, emotions and flesh lined up with this spiritual fact.

You might find it helpful to begin to think of yourself as a soldier in battle. Because you are no longer in Satan's army and he can no longer rule over your life, his goal for believers is to discourage them to keep them from being effective soldiers for God. Satan wants to see you negative, guilty and confused because when you are, you are no threat to him. One of Satan's main goals is to keep you living a life of defeat and confusion.

Back in 2006, in the mountains of Afghanistan, during the hunt for Osama Bin Laden, a platoon of British soldiers was stationed near the front line of the Taliban's forces. Being as they were in the mountains, far from any cities or civilization, the men were bored most of the time as they spent their days and nights searching through binoculars for caves where they thought Bin Laden might be hiding. Two weeks had passed and they had not spotted any movement at all. The men were becoming anxious and irritable.

Suddenly, during the night, a large unmarked crate was dropped in the distance. The men spotted it and thought it might be supplies, though they had not had contact with the helicopter. The next morning, they approached the crate carefully and inspected it. It had no markings. The major leading the platoon decided to open it. Inside the crate, the soldiers found bottles of Guinness Stout, Heineken and Russian vodka. Near the bottom of the crate, were bricks of drugs—both heroin and marijuana—playing cards, board games, potato chips, pretzels and snacks, bottles of water, cigarettes, fire crackers, poker chips, a cooler with packs of hotdogs and frozen steaks. The bored soldiers were elated and some began drinking the liquor without waiting for an okay from their commanders. The major ordered the crate shut until he could confirm where it came from, but no one within radio reach admitted to having delivered the contraband.

Eventually, the constant pressure from his bored platoon wore down the major's resistance. That night, the men threw a party. They drank, ate, and partied as if they were back in London. Despite the rules against it, they lit a small fire during the night to cook the hot dogs and steaks. By 2am, the entire platoon was intoxicated—including the major who managed to resist for three hours, but eventually gave in to the smell of a medium rare T-bone and a few swigs of Smirnoff vodka. At 3 am, the Taliban attacked and killed the entire platoon. They were defenseless in their state of intoxication. The crate had been left there by the Taliban to achieve that exact purpose. Osama Bin Laden was passing through and made his way safely into Pakistan.

Like Bin Laden, Satan knows he cannot recruit you to join his army. He knows you are his mortal enemy, but he also knows that if he can get you to forget who you are, or if he can make you ineffective, you won't cause any trouble for him. One of his best ways of making believers ineffective is to crush their spirits under the weight of guilt. He is called the "accuser of the brethren" for a reason. By whispering your guilt and failings in your ear, Satan can make you take your eyes off your mission and become completely ineffective for Jesus.

What Satan is saying is not true. When he tries to remind you of your past or present failings, he is simply trying to disarm you so he can make you ineffective. This is where the blood of Jesus is of absolute importance in your life. When you claim the blood of Jesus, you are reaffirming your standing as a forgiven believer in Jesus Christ. You are restating for yourself the fact of your position in Christ. When you claim the blood of Jesus, you release forgiveness over whatever Satan is accusing you of doing. You are telling Satan that you have been forgiven and he has no place, nor right to say otherwise.

A few years ago, a homeless man was invited as a guest of the Owner of Baltimore Ravens, Art Model, to attend a home football game. He arrived at the stadium in the best clothes he had—a raggedy and dirty jacket—but realized he had misplaced his pass.

He searched his jacket, his pants and all his belongings, but he could not find it. The security guards thought that the man was lying because he did not look like the other guests who regularly entered at the VIP gate on home game days. The man got upset— not wanting to miss the opportunity or the promised free meal. Other guards began arriving as back up to remove him. Two huge guards grabbed him beneath each arm and lifted him violently.

Humiliated and embarrassed, the man began kicking to be released. As he did, his VIP pass fell out from his pants leg. It had slipped through a hole in his pocket and lodged between the two pairs of pants he was wearing to keep warm. When the guards saw it fall out, they didn't want to release the man, but they recognized the pass. It was a special pass to the Ravens owner's private suite. They knew if they did not make sure this man got to that suite, they would lose their jobs. They apologized profusely, put the man down and made sure he got safely where he belonged.

The security guards were going to do whatever they wanted to do to that man until they realized he had a higher authority. That is what you have when you plead the blood of Jesus in your life. When you release the blood of Jesus, Satan has to release you.

The story is told of a man who dreamed of seeing the inside of the White House. One day, in 1998, he finally had enough money for the trip. He spent all he had on a bus ticket to Washington D.C.. When he arrived, he found out where the White House was and walked there from Union Station. However, when he arrived, he found out that the White House was closed to tours for three months due to repairs and he would not be able to see it. He begged for a chance to see it, but he was sternly refused. Saddened, defeated and with no money to return home, he walked across the street and sat on a bench and began to cry.

A young woman passing by noticed him crying and stopped to ask what was wrong. The man even refused to look up. Instead, he told her his sad story and how he had dreamed his whole life of seeing the inside of the White House. "You want to see inside the White House? Well, let's see what we can do about that. Follow me." The young woman walked across the street to the gate where the man had been turned back before. "It's no use, young lady, they won't let you in," the man said. But to his surprise, the marines opened the gate. Only then did the man realize he was being followed by two other men who accompanied the woman. As the man passed the Marine guard in disbelief, he heard him say, "Welcome back Ms. Clinton."

In our world, where status and power usually dictate how we are treated, it's no wonder we sometimes believe that our works or our individual achievements are more important than what Jesus did for us in the spiritual world. It is exactly this worldly perspective that Satan relies on to make us feel bad about our shortcomings or failings. The world may discard us for our weaknesses or shortcomings, but the opposite is true in Christ. Paul says in Philippians 3:3-9:

"We rely on what Christ Jesus has done for us. We put no confidence in human effort, ⁴though I could have confidence in my own effort if anyone could. Indeed, if others have

reason for confidence in their own efforts, I have even more!
[5]I was circumcised when I was eight days old. I am a pure-blooded citizen of Israel and a member of the tribe of Benjamin—a real Hebrew if there ever was one! I was a member of the Pharisees, who demand the strictest obedience to the Jewish law. [6]I was so zealous that I harshly persecuted the church. And as for righteousness, I obeyed the law without fault. [7]I once thought these things were valuable, but now I consider them worthless because of what Christ has done. [8]Yes, everything else is worthless when compared with the infinite value of knowing Christ Jesus my Lord. For his sake I have discarded everything else, counting it all as garbage, so that I could gain Christ [9]and become one with him. I no longer count on my own righteousness through obeying the law; rather, I become righteous through faith in Christ. For God's way of making us right with himself depends on faith."

As Paul says in the scriptures above, our righteousness is based solely on what Christ has done for us and the symbol of what Christ has done for us is the blood he shed on the cross. Therefore, when we plead the blood, we claim our righteousness in Jesus Christ and we show our VIP pass to Satan the accuser who wants to make us ineffective in our testimony. We show that we are operating under grace and not under our own authority or power. By releasing the blood of Jesus, we cover ourselves in God's authority and enter into the peace and power of forgiveness.

My sister, when you claim the blood of Jesus, you give yourself permission to make mistakes and to try again and again. There is nothing to be ashamed of. There is nothing to be guilty of. Our sins are forgiven. Hallelujah. And that forgiveness is eternal and infinite. The fight we fight day-by-day against the forces of evil is a fight to keep our minds and hearts in alignment with the truth that we are God's children—regardless of how we feel, how we look, or how we act. Despite ourselves or our own strength, we are God's children by birth through our faith in the death, burial and resurrection of Jesus Christ as our Lord and savior. We are covered in his righteousness—not our own. His blood purifies us from sin. We claim that blood to remind ourselves of our standing and place so that we do not give up or become discouraged in the process of becoming more like Christ. As Paul goes on to say in Philippians 3:12-14:

> *"12I don't mean to say that I have already achieved these things or that I have already reached perfection. But I press on to possess that perfection for which Christ Jesus first possessed me. 13No, dear brothers and sisters, I have not achieved it, but I focus on this one thing: Forgetting the past and looking forward to what lies ahead, 14I press on to reach the end of the race and receive the heavenly prize for which God, through Christ Jesus, is calling us."*

Our diligent work in growing closer to Jesus is not to save our souls or to make ourselves better fit for heaven. Our work is to be more like Christ. Our goal is to experience the life that Christ wants us to live. To do that, we must, like Paul, forget those things that are behind—the generational curses, the strongholds, the failings, the weaknesses and the doubts and to press on towards the life that God has for us.

PRAYER TO RELEASE THE BLOOD OF JESUS

Heavenly Father, I thank you for the forgiveness that was purchased for me on Calvary through the blood of your son Jesus Christ. I thank you that today and forever I stand before you holy and forgiven—cleansed from all sin and guilt. I declare your blood over my life now and ask you to help me remember that I am, and always will be, your child. You have promised never to leave me nor forsake me, so I am secure in my eternal relationship with you. When I struggle against my flesh, help to always remember who I am—that your son's blood covers me forever. Thank you for salvation. Thank you for being my father. Thank you for forgiveness and that my salvation is not dependent on my strength but on your mighty strength. In Jesus' name. Amen.

It is a wonderful thing to know that my salvation is not based on my strength. So many believers miss out on this important truth of our faith and instead believe they have to measure up or "earn their way" into heaven. But as Paul said, all our efforts to save ourselves are worthless, for "All have sin and fall short of the glory of God."

The truths I have shared with you throughout this book are nothing more than the scriptures God has left with us to guide us along our path. It's important that we learn these scriptures to help in guarding our minds daily against the attacks of the enemy. In the next chapter, we will examine how to know what God's word says about you and a special practice that has been a very powerful tool in my life—speaking God's truth about you to yourself. Have you ever noticed how so many times, people say things to us that can change our mood—lift us up and change our outlook on the day? When you speak God's truth about you to yourself, you find the power to lift yourself up even when there's no one else around to give you that word of encouragement.

Chapter 8

SPEAKING GOD'S TRUTH ABOUT YOU TO YOURSELF

"But he answered and said, It is written, Man shall not live by bread alone, but by every word that procee- deth out of the mouth of God." ~ Matthew 4:4

After we break the strongholds in our lives, another very powerful and helpful spiritual discipline for continuing to walk in victory is Speaking God's Truth About You to Yourself. I know this is kind of tricky wording, but the idea is not hard to understand. All I'm saying here is that you have to learn to practice positive (Bible based) self-talk.

We all know what self-talk is. That's when you're driving along minding your own business and you realize you forgot something. What usually happens in that moment is not just a mental exercise in which you quietly recall what you may have forgotten. Instead, most of us start talking to ourselves. "Girl, you know you forgot something. Did I? You know you did. What? I don't even know, but I know I forgot something." We've all been there. Sitting at the light, talking to ourselves. We might not be talking out loud—though I do all the time—but we're talking none the less. I have to admit that I really love the new Bluetooth wireless mobile phone and hands-free speaker systems they have out now. Now when someone sees me talking to myself, they assume I'm on a phone. It wasn't always like that. Driving down the street talking to myself doesn't even draw attention anymore. I used to find myself embarrassed at children staring at me and laughing. The other day, I saw a lady walking through the store just talking. Years ago, people might have called the police, but not anymore. It's wonderful.

The fact of the matter is that we are almost perpetually engaged in one form of self-talk or another. Whether we are working on projects we have to do or thinking about problems we're dealing with or going over what we want to make for dinner or what we plan to do on the weekend, our minds respond best to answering questions. Einstein said, "If I had 1 hour to solve the most important problem in the world, I would spend 55 minutes figuring out the right question to ask and 5 minutes finding the answer." And so it is that asking ourselves the right questions will often lead to the right answers.

One of the ways this really works is something I found in a book called *Awaken the Giant Within* by Anthony Robbins. In the book, Mr. Robbins says that the mind is used to providing answers to our questions whether the question is the right question or not. For instance, if you ask yourself a bad question like, "Why am I so stupid?" your mind will provide an answer to that question even though you are not stupid. If you ask that question, your mind is liable to reply, "Because your momma was stupid," or "you come from a stupid family," or "you've always been stupid," or "because you don't think." On and on it will go. It doesn't always stop to make sure you're asking a valid question.

So it's important that we force our mind to find positive answers for us by asking it positive and empowering questions. Instead of asking why am I so stupid, you might want to ask yourself something like, "How can I avoid making that mistake in the future?" Your mind will look for positive and constructive ways to help you, rather than some additional negative thing to put you down. For instance, the answer to that question might be, "write a note to yourself or put it in your phone's calendar" or "make sure to study at least one hour before the test next time."

In Robbins' book, he suggests you go even further by asking yourself empowering questions every day like, "What am I happy about today? What am I excited about today? How have I contributed to the world today? Who do I love? Who loves me? What did I learn today? What good thing can I celebrate today?" In fact, answer those questions for yourself right now. Expect that there is an answer—in other words, do not accept "no one" as an answer for who loves you. You are loved starting with Jesus, but I'm sure there are others as well. Watch how answering these questions lifts your spirit. They are empowering questions. These types of questions prime our mind with positive energy. Learning to ask these questions daily—Robbins suggests asking them right when you wake up every day and when you go to bed—will help you face your day with increased and powerful energy.

Similarly, throughout the day, we find ourselves engaged in conversations with ourselves that also have the power to encourage or discourage us. This is where speaking God's truth about ourselves to ourselves comes into play. The secret here is to learn some Word so we can have it handy when we need it. The Bible says that God's word is a "lamp unto our feet and a light unto our path." It also says:

Hebrews 4:12 - *For the word of God [is] quick, and powerful, and sharper than any two-edged sword, piercing even to the dividing asunder of soul and spirit, and of the joints and marrow, and [is] a discerner of the thoughts and intents of the heart.*

2 Timothy 3:16-17 - *All scripture [is] given by inspiration of God, and [is] profitable for doctrine, for reproof, for correction, for instruction in righteousness 17 That the man (and woman) of God may be perfect, thoroughly furnished unto all good works.*

Jeremiah 23:29 - *[Is] not my word like as a fire? saith the LORD; and like a hammer [that] breaketh the rock in pieces?*

Revelation 12:11 - *And they overcame him by the blood of the Lamb, and by the word of their testimony; and they loved not their lives unto the death.*

1 John 1:1 - *That which was from the beginning, which we have heard, which we have seen with our eyes, which we have looked upon, and our hands have handled, of the Word of life.*

Ephesians 6:17 - *And take the helmet of salvation, and the sword of the Spirit, which is the word of God.*

Romans 10:17 - *So then faith [cometh] by hearing, and hearing by the word of God.*

John 17:17 - *Sanctify them through thy truth: thy word is truth.*

John 6:63 - *It is the spirit that quickeneth; the flesh profiteth nothing: the words that I speak unto you, [they] are spirit, and [they] are life.*

Matthew 4:4 - *But he answered and said, It is written, Man shall not live by bread alone, but by every word that proceedeth out of the mouth of God.*

Isaiah 55:11 - *So shall my word be that goeth forth out of my mouth: it shall not return unto me void, but it shall accomplish that which I please,* *and it shall prosper [in the thing] whereto I sent it.*

Isaiah 40:8 - *The grass withereth, the flower fadeth: but the word of our God shall stand for ever.*

John 1:1-2 - *In the beginning was the Word, and the Word was with God, and the Word was God.*

Proverbs 30:5 - *Every word of God [is] pure: he [is] a shield unto them that put their trust in him.*

Deuteronomy 4:2 - *Ye shall not add unto the word which I command you, neither shall ye diminish [ought] from it, that ye may keep the command- ments of the LORD your God which I command you.*

Just go back and look at all the things the Bible says about itself. God's word is: pure, cannot be added to or subtracted from; was in the beginning; was with God; was God; will stand forever; achieves its goals; provides life; is truth; is like a hammer that breaks hard rocks into pieces; is quick and powerful and sharper than any two-edged sword; is profitable for doctrine and correc- tion; is a lamp to our feet; is a light to our path. In fact, both the longest chapter in the entire Bible and the longest Psalm, Psalm 119 in both cases, is entirely about God's word. Why does the Bible spend so much time talking about itself? Well, when God decided to speak to man through the generations, he used a book. God used words. But again why? Because, my sister, words are powerful.

Did you know that the word of God is the only offensive weapon in the Christian arsenal? Look at Paul's description of the armor of God in Ephesians 6:10-17:

> *Finally, be strong in the Lord and in his mighty power. Put on the full armor of God, so that you can take your stand against the devil's schemes. For our struggle is not against flesh and blood, but against the rulers, against the authorities, against the powers of this dark world and against the spiritual forces of evil in the heavenly realms. Therefore put on the full armor of God, so that when the day of evil comes, you may be able to stand your ground, and after you have done everything, to stand. Stand firm then, with the belt of truth buckled around your waist, with the breastplate of righteousness in place, and with your feet fitted with the readiness that comes from the gospel of peace. In addition to all this, take up the shield of faith, with which you can extinguish all the flaming arrows of the evil one. Take the helmet of salvation and the sword of the Spirit, which is the word of God.*

Here, Paul uses a picture of a Roman army officer, fully outfitted for war. The people of Israel during Jesus' day would have been very familiar with the site of a Roman officer, because Israel was occupied by Rome at that time. There were Roman army officers everywhere. Paul says we have to put on a spiritual type of armor in order to defend ourselves against "rulers, authorities and powers of this dark world and spiritual forces of evil in the heavenly realms." As we fight to break free of generational curses in our lives and the lives of our loved ones, we have to understand that we are also battling these same evil forces in the spiritual realm. But of all the armor of God—the belt of truth, breastplate of righteousness, the fitted feet of readiness, the shield of faith, the helmet of salvation and the sword of the Spirit, which is the Word of God—only one is an offensive weapon used to attack the enemy. The rest are defensive protections against the enemy's attack.

When you use God's word you are launching an attack in the spiritual realm against the forces of evil that seek to entrap, confuse, discourage, devalue, enslave, defeat, frustrate, and hurt you and your family.

People often fail to realize the power of words. Words can transform or destroy people—that old adage "sticks and stones may break my bones, but words will never hurt me," isn't quite true. Words have hurt many people. Words have started wars. Words have destroyed marriages. Words have ended friendships. Words have killed. God said, "Let there be light" and there was light. He has given us the power to create with our words as well. Before Muhammad Ali became the greatest, he was telling the whole world that he was the greatest. Today he is known as the greatest boxing legend of all time. He used words to transform himself and what others thought about him.

On the other hand, many frustrated parents and grandparents passed curses onto their children and family members by speaking negative words to them. The mother who calls their child stupid or dumb or ignorant, is not aware how ignorant she is being herself.

Children absorb what we say and often become the very things we call them. Mothers, fathers, caretakers and siblings often say the meanest things to their children. They may pass it off as joking or say "you know I'm just playing," but the child doesn't know that. What's more, the words are already out there. Negative words can hit people like a moving train—the one word can bring 15 more boxcars full of pain behind it. Therapists say that for every negative comment we hear, we have to hear 15 positives ones just to neutralize it. Just stopping a moving train takes a long time. It may take 5-10 more positive comments to get the emotional train moving in the positive direction.

One child I know was playing in the sprinkler during a hot summer day with his friends. A number of the children in the neighborhood were a little overweight, this child included. He heard his much older sister laugh and say to his mother, "He needs a training bra." For most of that child's life he believed he had breasts and was ashamed to go swimming with friends, get sprinkled, or take his shirt off in public. It took years after he was married before he realized his sister did not know what she was talking about. He made an appointment to see a plastic surgeon about male breast reduction surgery. The surgeon had him disrobe, he looked at him and asked, "Surgery for what? I wish I had your muscular chest. Men come here to have me give them what you have naturally." His sister's careless words had made him hate himself for years—even his own wife's appreciation of his body did nothing to help him feel better. The doctor's reassuring words finally broke through the years of mental anguish.

When we say negative cruel (even joking) things to children, we impact on them in their delicate years and often leave wounds that manifest years later in negative behavior. Call a child sneaky, devious, evil, crazy, stupid, dummy, idiot, sissy, a liar, a dog, a bi**h, a pimp, a little hustler, a fighter, a problem, a pain in the a**, a player, a punk, a whore, a criminal, a thief, a as*hole, or any other horrible negative name and you risk imprinting that child with an message that will repeat throughout their lives until they manifest it as teenagers and adults. This is another reason why the use of the N*word in songs is so horrible. All types of people, even some who should know better, argue that there is nothing wrong, that the word no longer means what it used to mean and that it's just a changing culture and it's lost its power. But let a child call himself that vile and nasty word long enough and one day he will start to think of himself as an N*word. Then, one day, he will be in a college history class, watch some historical documentary or read a history book and see how disgusting, evil, vile and hurtful that word was. He will read that word in its original context, and all the curse behind it, and he will hear himself calling himself that word—that is when it will hit him. That's when the horren-dous effect of the normalization of that word will kick in. If they stay ignorant of history all of their lives, maybe it won't have that effect—but that's even worse. No, my sister, save your loved one's life today. Control your tongue and help those around you to control their tongues.

Instead, call your children and loved ones smart, brilliant, beautiful, handsome, perfect, wonderful, intelligent, creative, amazing, powerful, talented, gifted, genius, strong, capable, responsible, loving, thoughtful, kind, wise, inventive, unique, and lovable and they will become all those things both as children and later as adults. Instead of looking for the negative things they do and opting for punishment and criticism, look for the positive things they do and opt for praise. Become a treasure hunter for praise. Dig as deep as you have to dig to find something good to say about those you love and care about the most and you will be rewarded with something worth far more than gold, my sister.

When you use negative words, you turn the tremendous creative power of words that God gives you against yourself and others. The Bible tells us in Romans 12:2 though that, as believers, we are to be transformed by the renewing of our minds. When our minds are renewed, our words should be renewed as well. Where we might have been used to cussing people out when they cut us off in traffic, which gives rise to anxiety, frustration and anger in us, our new minds should be able to stay calm, appreciate, and thank God for the fact that at least we avoided an accident. This type of thinking brings peace, appreciation, empowerment, joy and strength. Go even further and thank God you have a car to drive, the ability to drive, and the money to drive and afford a car. Where you used to blow up, when you become a treasure hunter of praise, you will mellow out and find joy in every waking hour. If you're in your right mind, praise God. If you can see this page, praise God. If you have the ability to read these words, praise God. If you got enough education to understand what I'm telling you right now, praise God. If the breath is going in and out of your lungs right now, praise God. If it's going in and out of your lungs without the help of a big machine, praise God even more.

My sister, when you start to look, you will find reasons to praise God all around you every single second of every single day. And if you look hard enough, you will find a reason to praise your children, praise your spouse, praise your family member, your loved one, your friend. When you become a treasure hunter for praise, you'll even find ways to praise yourself. "Hey, I didn't go off on that woman who gave me that bad attitude at the DMV— well, praise me for that! I didn't repay evil for evil. I was compassionate. I avoided spite. I was kind. I was encouraging. I'm alright. I'm good peeps."

Renewing your mind means doing something new. If it's the old way you've always done something, rethink it and see if there is a new way to do it that lines up more with God's word. If you catch yourself in your old mindset, ask how you can demonstrate your new mind instead. How could I have handled that in a kinder, gentler way? The question many people have said and suggested for this is "What would Jesus do?" Some people even put little W.W.J.D. bracelets on their wrists to remind them to ask that question. Whether you chose to do this or not, become a treasure hunter of praise and you will automatically begin to speak more powerfully into your loved ones lives, your co-workers lives, your friends and even your own life. You will not only transform your own life, but you will become a transformer—speaking life, power, love, encouragement and joy to everyone you meet.

As your only offensive weapon, knowing the word of God as it applies to you is very important. When you speak God's word to yourself, you remind yourself of your relationship in God's family and God's promises to protect you and your loved ones. I have found it a very helpful practice to keep a pen and paper handy. Whenever I come across a verse in the Bible that says something about me or my relationship to God, to jot it down and keep these little notes in a jar near my desk. I often go to this jar when I need a little pick me up during the day and read one of the statements aloud. Here is a sample of just a few:

We are of a royal priesthood. 1 Peter 2:9

We are the righteousness of God in Him. 2 Corinthians. 5:21

I can do all things through Christ who strengthens me. Philippians. 4:13

The LORD will make you the head and not the tail, and you only will be above, and you will not be underneath. Duet. 28:13

Beloved, I pray that in all respects you may prosper and be in good health, just as your soul prospers. 3 Jn.1:2

We are more than conquerors through him who loved us. Rom 8:37

As I read these statements and promises, I thank God for my relationship with him and my position in his family. When the devil tries to attack me or when I'm feeling weak, sad, frustrated or down, in addition to reaching for my Bible, I can reach for my little jar of affirmations to give a quick lift to my spirit. If you are technically savvy and want an easy way to access God's word anytime, make sure to go to ITunes, Google Play or the Windows app store to download any number of free Bible apps that will give you a daily scripture and a bit of God's word to read and think about each day. You can even find specific Bible promise apps to point you to an encouraging scripture anytime you open them. Many of these apps even come with a reminder feature to make sure you take time each day to read God's word and learn more about his promises so that you become fluent in speaking God's truth about you to yourself.

My sister, positive verbalization counters automatic negative verbalization and thinking that accompanies difficult situations. Where you may have once confessed all the bad things that could go wrong when faced with challenges, which often lead to guilt, shame, fear, defeat and self-doubt, look to these scriptures and the practice of Speaking God's Truth about You to Yourself to develop a new, positive, trusting, victorious attitude in the face of negative circumstances. As these scriptures are God's word, they carry the weight of God's presence and help motivate growth rather than perpetuate defeat. The more your practice this principle of speaking God's truth to yourself, your level of trust and commitment to God's word will grow and you will better understand God and his will and plan for your life. When you renew your mind, you "surrender to the Holy Spirit" and he begins a transformation in you that is lasting, ever-expanding and which leads to the ultimate joy and contentment God wants you to have in your life.

Chapter 9

OBEDIENCE—THE ACCESS TO YOUR SUCCESS

*"Delight yourself in the Lord, and he will give you
the desires of your heart." ~Psalm 37:4*

My sister, we've come a long way on our journey together though God's word. You've made it to the last regular chapter of the book. By the way, do you know that most people who buy a book and start to read it never get past the first few chapters? So your making it this far is a real accomplishment. Congratulations! Yay for you! The final chapter is just review, so this is the final thought I want to share with you.

The last spiritual lesson that will help us to keep our lives free from curse and create blessing and power in our lives and our family's lives for years to come is to practice obedience to God's Word.

Throughout the Bible, believers are admonished to obey the word of God. Obedience is necessary for maintaining your life on this new path of freedom and keeping curses from reestablishing themselves both in your life and in the lives of your loved ones.

Take a look at the these verses from the Bible:

"Behold, I set before you this day a blessing and a curse: A blessing, if you obey the commandment of the Lord your God, which I command you this day: And a curse, if you will not obey the commandments of the Lord your God."   *Deut. 11:26-28*

And all these blessings shall come upon you and overtake you, because you obey the voice of the Lord your God. Blessed shall you be in the city, and blessed shall you be in the country. Blessed shall be the fruit of your body, the produce of your ground and the increase of your herds, the increase of your cattle and the offspring of your flocks. Blessed shall be your basket and your kneading bowl. Blessed shall you be when you come in, and blessed shall you be when you go out. The Lord will cause your enemies who rise against you to be defeated before your face; they shall have come out against you one way and flee before you seven days.   *Deut. 28:2:14*

You should notice right away that God has already set up the rules of the game so that blessings follow obedience to his Word and curses follow disobedience. It truly makes no sense to go through all of this book and learn all of these techniques for freeing your life and your family's lives from generational curses if you only turn around and pull down new problems.

Think of it like this. There are bankruptcy laws in the United States that are based on the Bible's teaching of the forgiveness of debt every 7 years. In the Bible, a debt could only stay on a person for 7 years. After that, the debt was to be forgiven. Here's the verse:

"At the end of every seven years you must cancel debts. 2 This is how it is to be done: Every creditor shall cancel the loan he has made to his fellow Israelite. He shall not require payment from his fellow Israelite or brother, because the LORD's time for canceling debts has been proclaimed." ~Deuteronomy 15:1-2.

Because this law was in the Bible, a form of it was adopted into American law as well. Now, if you find yourself in debt and unable to pay it, you have the right to declare bankruptcy every 7 years. Unfortunately, it ruins your credit, but at least you don't have to go to debtor's prison or become someone's slave because of debts. (Of course, depending on how you feel about your job, that's debatable—still, you're not a slave even if you hate your job—you are always free to step out on faith and try something else. I'm not recommending you do that without serious thought and prayer, but my point is that you don't have to stay there.) But imagine if you get into financial trouble or you do something irresponsible and find you can't pay your bills. If you take advantage of the bankruptcy laws and have your debts forgiven, it would be wise for you to use that opportunity to improve your credit and to be wiser in your spending in the future. You were fortunate to be forgiven, so be wiser and more careful so that you don't have to have ruined credit again once you get your new start.

In some ways, breaking free of generational guilt is a bit like being forgiven your debt. Does that mean you can't go on the same shopping sprees you used to go on? Probably. After all, if that's what led to excessive debt, it is wise to not do it again even though it may be hard. Maybe you will have to skip buying some things. Save more. Spend less. Budget better. No, it may not be as fun, but it is also not as embarrassing or humiliating. Likewise, it may be harder to obey God, but it is much better than living with new problems because you ignore his word.

It's also like a drug addict or alcoholic getting sober. Once you get sober, it's important that you avoid the drugs or alcohol in the future. Obedience is how we avoid those things that lead to generational curse in our lives.

I can hear you now, "But it's so hard to obey all the time." It can be, but it doesn't have to be. There are certain practices that make obedience to God a lot easier or a lot harder. Practicing the principles we discussed earlier in the book will help you put the odds in your favor. By keeping your mind positive, thinking on

God's Word, and repeating his word to yourself, you will gradually grow closer to God and find yourself more able to make wise, powerful, godly decisions in your day-to-day life. Obedience is the key to developing greater trust in God and a greater natural desire to obey God.

Now I might hear you saying something else, "But sister Patricia, there's so many rules. How can I obey them all? Isn't that asking too much?"

I'm going to give you a little secret that I find so powerful and liberating, which most believers still don't understand, even though it is so clearly revealed in the Bible and people quote it all the time. I'll bet you've even heard of it. The way I use it helps obedience become almost second nature for us. It is the secret key to all the power, grace and wisdom you need to walk with God and please him every day of your life. If you follow this one teaching, you won't have to worry about ever displeasing God again.

What is it?

It's a little story tucked away in the book of Matthew, Chapter 22 verses 34-40. Here it is.

"When the Pharisees heard that he had silenced the Sadducees with his reply, they met together to question him again. One of them, an expert in religious law, tried to trap him with this question: "Teacher, which is the most important commandment in the law of Moses?"

Jesus replied, 'You must love the Lord your God with all your heart, all your soul, and all your mind.' This is the first and greatest commandment. A second is equally important: 'Love your neighbor as yourself.' The entire law and all the demands of the prophets are based on these two commandments."

Do you see it, sister? It is the secret to pleasing God summed up in a few simple words. Maybe this other verse from the Old Testament will help you see it better:

"People, the LORD has told you what is good, and this is what he requires of you: to do justice, to love mercy, and to walk humbly with your God." ~Micah 6:8

Do you think you can do that sister? Look at how simple it is. God's not asking you to memorize the whole Bible. He's not asking you to go to Bible college. He's not asking you to devote your life to ministry or to spend your whole day reading his word. He's summed it all up in two different places in such simple and clear terms that it makes the whole thing make so much sense. The entire Bible, Jesus says, the WHOLE LAW and ALL THE DEMANDS OF THE PROPHETS all spring from these two simple commands: "Love the Lord your God with your heart, mind and soul, and love your neighbor as yourself." Micah put it this way, "Do justice, love mercy and walk humbly."

Oh, you should be jumping in your seat right now, sister. If those verses free your heart like they freed mine when I first understood them, you should be feeling so much relief, so much power, so much love and so much joy that it's hard to contain it all. Look at those verses again. They are so powerful.

Now here's the big secret of Jesus' answer. He was asked, "What is THE MOST important commandment?" Jesus answered with the answer, AND the way to know you're practicing the answer. The first and most important is to "love the Lord with all your heart and soul and mind." Wow. That sounds complicated. How do you even do that? That's a heavy command. How do I know I'm doing that? How can I be sure I love him with all my heart and soul and mind? That's not easy, right? WRONG! He throws in the second commandment to help clarify the first. How do you know you love the Lord your God with all your heart, soul and mind? You know when you "love your neighbor as yourself." That's what Micah means too: "Do justice (that's to your neighbor), love mercy (that's to your neighbor) and walk humbly with God (that's automatic when you're doing justice and loving mercy.) Think about it. Can you do justice and love mercy and not walk humbly? Of course not. The whole reason you care to do justice and love mercy is because you are walking humbly with God. What makes you merciful? The fact that God was merciful to you—that's what. What makes you do justice (fairness), because you love God and want to please him. It's all connected, sister.

You know you love God with all your heart, mind and soul when you love your neighbor as yourself. You know you're walking humbly with God when you do justice and love mercy. Do you see it now, sister? The power of God's word all summed up in such simple language. You could even look at it like this "Just be good to each other." "Treat everyone as you would want them to treat you." Not as they treat you—but as you "want them to treat you." With mercy. With fairness. With love. I bet you've heard it called the "Golden Rule." That's why it's golden. That's why it's so important.

Hallelujah! Hallelujah! Praise Jesus. It's not so complicated. It's all so simple and you know this is truth in your soul as you read it. Your soul, God's spirit living in your soul says, "Yes!"

This is liberation, not bondage. This is power, not weakness. This is joy, not pain. This is love, not duty. This is mercy, grace, peace.

And, if you look around, this is what seems to be missing most in our world. When we see people and politicians who claim to be Christians and followers of Jesus, we often see judgmental, intolerant people bent on making other people do what they want them to do. We do not see mercy; instead, we see judgment. We don't see justice; instead, we see bombings, killings and cheating. We don't see humility; instead, we see arrogance, rebellion, racism and attitudes of superiority.

How many people do you honestly see who live their lives with the thought of "what would Jesus do?" Very few. In fact, when I see some of the people who claim they are Christians— particularly those in the public light—I have to ask myself what Jesus they're talking about. In fact, I just saw something posted on a friend's Facebook page from comedian Stephen Colbert that kind of sums up with I'm saying. Colbert said, "If this is going to be a Christian nation that doesn't help the poor, either we've got to pretend that Jesus was just as selfish as we are, or we've got to acknowledge that he commanded us to love the poor and serve the needy without condition and then admit that we just don't want to do it."

And that's why so many of us are under a curse, my sister. When it comes to the teachings of Jesus, many of us just don't want to do it. We imagine it's harder than it is to love the needy, to care for others, to be kind, do justice and love mercy—to treat everyone we meet in the same way we want to be treated.

But can you imagine what the world would be like if people actually did that? What if the banker, the shopkeeper, the corporation, the salesperson, the clerk, the attendant, the manager, and the advertiser all treated people the way they themselves wanted to be treated? What if politicians didn't lie, because they didn't want us to lie to them? What if stores didn't cheat us on prices, because they didn't want anyone to cheat them? What if police treated every young black man they come in contact with as if they were their supervisors or family members—at least as human beings—treated them as they wanted to be treated? What if no one stole, because they didn't want to be stolen from? What if no one killed, because they didn't want to be killed? All of this could happen if Christians just took Jesus seriously.

I know I'm asking for a lot to see such a drastic change in our world, but you have to understand that any change we see at all starts with us. If you want to see change in your life and your family's lives, you've got to change what you're doing. If you want to see curses broken never to return again, you've got to change that pattern today. It starts with you, sister. It starts with you taking Jesus seriously—taking the Lord at his word. It starts with you trusting him, obeying him.

The more we walk with him, the more change we'll see in our lives and the lives of family members. The more change we see in our lives, the more change we'll see in our neighborhoods. The more change we see in our neighborhoods, the more we'll see in our cities. The more we see in our cities, the more we'll see in our states. The more we see in our states, the more we'll see in our nation. The more we see in our nation, the more we'll see in the world. It really does start with you. It starts with you right now.

I trust that you've already decided to make these changes and already begun to break, or have even already broken, free of generational curse. But if you're still on the fence when it comes to obedience, let me share one other thing.

Many times, we think that it's going to take so much to make a change in our lives. As I write this, it is nearing the holiday season—just a week before Thanksgiving. Soon it will be New Years and that's when so many people decide (or say they are deciding) to make a change in their lives—they start new diets, they make new plans, they resolve to live better, be better. So many people put these new plans off for the future as if there is some magic in the future. If you want to work out and get into shape, why are you waiting for the future to do it? If you say you're too busy now, then what makes you think you won't be too busy in the future? Studies tell us this is one of the most basic flaws of human nature. We always think that our future selves will be more disciplined, more focused, more responsible, more diligent or more efficient than our current self. But it's just not true. If you're going to start a diet—don't wait, do it now—otherwise, you probably won't. If you're going to write a book, don't wait until you get a new computer, a new desk, a new notebook, new pens, or whatever. You don't need any of that. Those things are all just excuses. If you want to write a book, write one. Now. If you don't, you probably won't.

Here's a little secret—all change happens instantly. We often think that it takes time for people to change, but that's not really true. What takes time is deciding to change. Once you decide, you change in an instant.

You know what I'm talking about. You think about quitting a job and getting another one for a year or two before you do it. You might be weighing the benefits and negatives. You might be trying to figure out if you're making a mistake or not. You might be wondering if you'll find another job. Or maybe you're just waiting for that last straw that's going to break the camel's back. But once you decide you're quitting, it happens very quickly. Once you make that decision, it's as good as done.

You're decision to walk in obedience to the Lord shouldn't really be anything you have to think about. It is, after all, commanded of every believer. Usually, what we're thinking about when we think about obedience is how much fun we might miss out on. I suggest to you that you won't miss out on any fun. Jesus came to give you life and life more abundantly, not more blandly.

He's not interested in you losing your joy. That's not his goal and it won't be your experience. When you walk in obedience to Christ, you will find joy you never knew existed and a peace that surpasses understanding.

My sister, obedience seals the blessings of God in your life. The Bible says in Psalm 37:4, "Delight yourself in the Lord, and he will give you the desires of your heart." I pray you are encouraged to continue to follow his path for your life. Not only so that you won't experience curse anymore, but so that you will experience life more abundantly and so that you will have the desires of your heart.

CHAPTER 10

CONCLUSION

"Therefore, since we are surrounded by such a huge
crowd of witnesses to the life of faith, let us strip off
every weight that slows us down, especially the sin that
so easily trips us up. And let us run with endurance
the race God has set before us." ~Hebrews 12:1

Well, you did it. You made it to the final chapter. Congratulations. I pray that you have enjoyed our time together. The experiences and wisdom I've shared with you in this book have come from a long life of walking with the Lord. As you can tell, I've been through a lot. But God has been faithful. Times I thought I should have given up, he's brought me through. Likewise, you made it through. Maybe there were times you thought you should give up on finishing this book—although I certainly hope not, resistance can be a strong adversary. Nonetheless, you did not give up and here you are standing with me at the finish line.

In the introduction to this book, I mentioned the tragic story of Whitney Houston and her daughter Bobbi Kristina who both overdosed and died much too young. They are not alone. Singer Chris Brown severely beat singer Rihanna only hours before the two were to attend the Grammys together. Later, they were back together. The list of people who have attained remarkable success only to find themselves fighting with the demons of generational curse goes on and on.

The immensely successful King of Pop, Michael Jackson, needed a cocktail of drugs just so he could sleep at night and eventually died from an overdose of tranquilizers generally used on horses. The overwhelming evidence of his inability to love how God created him is chronicled as having been directly passed to him by a father who repeatedly mocked his appearance as a young boy. Just this year, the singer Prince was found having overdosed on pain killers as well. Prince's father was allegedly very strict and kicked him out of the house as a young man. Chaka Khan, who has battled drugs most of her life, is reportedly back in rehab.

Moreover, do not forget the famous and talented actor from the Batman Dark Knight movie, Heath Ledger who also over-dosed. Academy Award for best actor winner, Philip Seymour Hoffman overdosed on heroin. And just this past year, a winner of every award imaginable and a man who made millions of people laugh with delight, Robin Williams committed suicide. In the wake of Williams' suicide, comedian, actor and TV host, Wayne Brady, who also makes us all laugh, admitted that he, too, often had thoughts of suicide.

It is not just the rich and famous who suffer generational curses that destroy their lives despite their tremendous success. There are plenty of us common, everyday folk who deal with similar issues. In some of the more serious cases, medical attention is needed to help balance out brain chemistry that can be askew. Williams and others used medication, but were ultimately unable to overcome their issues. But even with medical attention, we have to learn the techniques to help quiet and eliminate the negativity in our lives and break the curses that can be passed down through our genetics by parents, grandparents and others over generations.

This process begins with purpose. I can't get into Whitney Houston's mind and tell you what she believed her purpose was— perhaps she thought it was to sing, make a lot of money, or party. What I do know is that she did not understand her purpose the way that God intended.

Contrary to popular belief, men and women are not put on this planet just to get rich and famous, drive around in nice cars, live in fine homes and indulge in all that their hearts desire. Men and women are created to know God first and foremost. If you don't know God first and foremost in your life, your purpose can easily be confused by the world's values—the values of Madison Avenue, Hollywood and what other people think.

Living a life of purpose requires a focused mind. It's not enough to just have stuff—stuff is fine, but stuff will not fulfill you. A focused mind will know that stuff cannot be the center of a life if you want that life to be fulfilling. God wants to know you. He wants you to know him. It is fine that you pursue the things you want in life, but God wants to be there with you, sharing his power, wisdom, grace, and values with you.

Had Whitney Houston understood her purpose, she would have understood her role as protector of her child. Rather than indulging in the selfish behavior of drugs, she would have recognized the consequences of her actions and taken the necessary steps to make right choices. She would have known how to pray and seek the power of God through faith to intervene in her life to break the cycle of generational dysfunction and curse.

Whitney certainly understood the role of resistance in helping to build her voice and career. Performers understand the need to rehearse songs, practice singing, train their voice to do what they want it to do, and master musicality and performance so that the audience enjoys the show. Practice, practice, practice—to ensure the performance goes as planned and fans continue to stay fans. Singers must eat right to stay healthy and maintain their bodies. They must discipline their minds to overcome mental resistance, which may spring up when they have to perform a song they've sung one hundred times this year. Whitney understood how to overcome the resistance she faced in her job as a top singer, actor and model. Nevertheless, what Whitney did not seem to understand is that resistance comes in many other forms outside of our work.

The devil, according to the Bible, roams throughout the world seeking whom he can destroy. So many times, we believe that all we need is worldly success to make our way in the world. But generational curse doesn't care how successful you are. Generational curse can push past your security gate, your alarm and your iron doors. Generational curse can get around your therapist, your wife and your guard dog. Understanding that generational curse may have been active in her life would have helped Whitney to be on guard for its many attacks and helped her stay grounded in her faith and life so that she did not give into the temptations that help generational curse achieve its goal of destroying life.

Had Whitney understood the concept of Synchronizing her Faith to God's word, she would have understood that everything that happened to her worked together for her good. Whatever you are going through, God is going through it with you. He is there. He never leaves you and never forsakes you. Therefore, you can say with confidence, the Lord is my helper, I will not be afraid. Whatever it is, there is a good and perfect solution when you synchronize your faith with God's word. God is always present. Always loving. Always forgiving. Always able and always willing to help.

Having the knowledge of what generational curses are and how they can affect one's life would have given Whitney more insight into her issues. So many times, we can be plagued with unexplainable issues that repeatedly show up in our journey. Knowledge that such things may well be passed down from ancestors would have helped her prepare to rid her life and her family of these curses. Instead, her inaction most likely guaranteed that Bobbi Kristina would grow up dealing with deep issues only multiplied by her mother's overdose.

Had Whitney understood that generational curse existed in her life, she could have then repented and asked God to intervene in destroying the curse over her life. She could have used the techniques of chapter 4-7 to not only identify the curse, but recognize that as a believer, she had the power to break it. Furthermore, she could have destroyed the strongholds that may have been fixed in her life by avoiding the places and activities that trigger and activate the curse or empower it. Ultimately, she would have understood how to release the all-powerful blood of Jesus over herself and her family's life so that no violence or weapon formed against them would prosper.

Throughout this process of breaking free of generational curse, Whitney would understand and know the power and privilege of speaking God's word about herself to herself. She would have gained the confident reassurance that God's word gives us when we meditate on it. Rather than giving into her emotion or depression or weakness, which left her seeking drugs in a hotel room in Beverly Hills, she could have found the peace and comfort of knowing that God loves her and that God would care for her emotionally, mentally and spiritually.

Ultimately, Whitney would have learned to walk in obedience in order to find the true success that her soul desired. Rather than feeling a need to seek escape to resolve her issues, she would have known that she had the full power of God available to her to help her overcome her troubles and walk victoriously not just in her professional career, but in where it truly matters—in her soul.

Because you have made it this far, I trust you long ago committed yourself to trusting Jesus Christ as your savior and committed yourself to the process of breaking generational curses in your own life and in your family's life. If by some chance, you've made it this far into this book and still have not made up your mind, don't leave this page without doing it right now.

Here is a prayer to commit your life to Christ and break the curse over your family's lives and your life:

Lord Jesus, I thank you for your sacrifice on the cross for my sins and allowing me to become your child. As your child, I am a new creature. I recognize that there are negative issues, habits and curses in my life that I have failed to overcome on my own and that may well have been passed down from my foreparents to me. I desire to break curses now. I plead the blood of Jesus over my life and my family's life now knowing that the blood of Jesus paid the price for all the sins of the world. These curses are broken over my life and the lives of my loved ones right now. All strongholds are demolished and forbidden from ever being reestablished in our lives. I thank you for that power. I thank you for breaking these curses. I ask you to help me remember to speak your word to myself and to my family always and stay close to you. In Jesus' name I pray. Amen.

My sister, we've come to the end of our journey together. If this book has blessed you, please share it with others and please take a moment and send me an email or tweet or a message on Facebook to let me know. It has been my great pleasure sharing the lessons I've learned on my journey thus far with the Lord. I pray this book be a blessing to you and your loved ones and all who read it for many years to come.

—Patricia Barrington, N.Y.C.

BREAKING GENERATIONAL CHAINS—A WOMAN'S GUIDE TO FREEDOM WORKBOOK

Directions: Please answer the following questions.

CHAPTER 1: KNOWING YOUR PURPOSE: LIFE AND CALLING

1) In what ways have personal actions and behaviors influenced your family and sphere of influence? Have you always made a good impression on those around you?

_____

_____

_____

_____

_____

_____

_____

_____

_____

_____

2) What is the first step in overcoming generational curses?

_____

_____

_____

_____

_____

_____

_____

_____

_____

3) List three consequences that generational curses can have on your family. Are any of these consequences present in your family?

_____

_____

_____

_____

_____

_____

_____

_____

_____

4) What bondage are you in today? (self-pity, addictions, over-eating, emotional eating, anxiety, etc.) Have you become comfortable in your bondage?

_____

_____

_____

_____

_____

_____

_____

_____

_____

5) How have your personal attitudes and beliefs contributed to repeated cycles of failure?

_____

_____

_____

_____

_____

_____

_____

_____

_____

Prayer Starter: Father God, in the name of Jesus, please expose the generational curses that are in operation in my family. Lord, show me areas of my life where these curses have influenced me. I decide today that I am ready to be healed. Please walk me through this deliverance as I surrender my pain in exchange for your freedom. Amen.

Chapter Challenge:

CHAPTER 2: WHY IS THIS HAPPENING?
WHAT AM I DOING AND WHY?

1) How can you overcome ignorance? Has ignorance stopped you from pursuing and achieving your goals?

_____

_____

_____

_____

_____

_____

_____

_____

2) What was the last goal you attempted to accomplish but didn't follow through? What type of RESISTANCE did you encounter?

_____

_____

_____

_____

_____

_____

_____

_____

3) What is logical resistance? How can you overcome it?

_____

_____

_____

_____

_____

_____

_____

_____

_____

4) What steps did the author take in achieving her goal to go to Ethiopia? What steps can you take to achieve yours?

_____

_____

_____

_____

_____

_____

_____

_____

_____

5) What is the subtlest way that resistance manifests itself in your life? Have you experienced this manifestation? If so, what has it stopped you from doing?

_____

_____

_____

_____

_____

_____

_____

_____

_____

_____

Prayer Starter: Father God, in the name of Jesus, please grant me revelation to understand your spiritual truths for my life. If I have operated in ignorance, I repent. Please show me how to utilize what you have placed on the inside of me for your glory. In Jesus' name, Amen.

Chapter Challenge:

CHAPTER 3: SYNCHRONIZING YOUR FAITH

1) No matter what has happened in your life, what promise does God's word provide about your outcome? Provide a scriptural reference.

_____

_____

_____

_____

_____

_____

_____

_____

2) What are the top three areas in your life that you are struggling with? List a scripture for each area.

_____

_____

_____

_____

_____

_____

_____

_____

_____

3) Define the word "synchronize." Now, define the word "faith."

_____

_____

_____

_____

_____

_____

_____

_____

_____

_____

4) List the five step plan the author mentioned that will help you synchronize your faith with God's word.

_____

_____

_____

_____

_____

_____

_____

_____

_____

_____

5) Why is scripture meditation so important? What do you benefit from it? When was the last time you meditated on God's word continuously?

_____

_____

_____

_____

_____

_____

_____

_____

_____

_____

Prayer Starter: Father God, in the name of Jesus, I ask you Lord to lead me and guide me into all truth. Give me the discipline that I need to meditate on your word. Allow Your Word to penetrate deep within my heart, into the depths of my soul. Allow my faith to synchronize with your Word. In Jesus' name, Amen.

Chapter Challenge:

CHAPTER 4: WHAT ARE GENERATIONAL CURSES?

1. This chapter referenced various types of "curses" that affect people. Based on the information presented, can you identify anything that might be a curse in your life, which you want to remove?

_____

_____

_____

_____

_____

_____

_____

_____

2. Do you see any behaviors in yourself that you also notice in one of your parents/grandparents/siblings that you do not like?

_____

_____

_____

_____

_____

_____

_____

_____

_____

3. Are there any behaviors you do that could be classified as bad habits that you want to break because they are hindering you by stealing your time, energy, money, joy or other valuable resources?

_____

_____

_____

_____

_____

_____

_____

_____

_____

4. Does your family suffer from any long-time or intergenerational diseases?

_____

_____

_____

_____

_____

_____

_____

_____

_____

5. Nearly everyone in America struggles with issues related to money or the love of money. Do you see any ways in which the love of money is an issue for you and or your family? For instance, is your spending under control? Do you live within your means or do you only make it because of credit cards and other debt?

_____

_____

_____

_____

_____

_____

_____

_____

_____

Prayer Starter: Lord God, I come to you in the name of your son, Jesus Christ, seeking help and guidance as I begin to identify and get free from generational curses that have plagued my family for years. I know that you want the curse to stop with me, so I submit my will to yours. Please open my eyes to any and all issues that may have hindered my family members or me. Where I lack the will or strength, give me the will and strength to confront these issues and overcome them. Break all curses in my life through this process of fellowship, discovery and study. Give me the wisdom and courage to see not only the negative impact of my past actions, but the power and freedom available to me in following your path.

Thank you for leading me on this path of growth and empowerment. In Jesus' name. Amen.

Chapter Challenge:

CHAPTER 5: BREAKING GENERATIONAL CURSES

1. Do you sometimes feel like something is wrong in your life but you cannot verbalize what is wrong?

_____

_____

_____

_____

_____

_____

_____

_____

_____

2. What are these two Scriptures saying about Knowledge and truth? Hosea 4:6 and John 8:32, 36

_____

_____

_____

_____

_____

_____

_____

_____

_____

3. What does James 5:16 say we must do in order to be healed?

_____

_____

_____

_____

_____

_____

_____

_____

_____

4. Why do we want these curses to be broken off our lives?

_____

_____

_____

_____

_____

_____

_____

_____

_____

5. What do you understand about yourself, your value and your relationship to God now that you did not understand before and how does that affect your view of yourself?

_____

_____

_____

_____

_____

_____

_____

_____

_____

_____

Prayer Starter: Heavenly Father, I come before you in the name of my Lord and Savior Jesus Christ. I praise and thank you for the redemptive power of the blood of Jesus, **who has redeemed us from the power of the law.** I confess all sins that have given the enemy legal right to operate any curse on my household and me. Father, Jesus said in John 14 **if I ask any thing in His name You would do it.** So, Father, I repent and ask You to forgive me for any ways, thoughts, deeds and actions that have brought me to this point in my life. Please remove and destroy all curses, word curses and generational curses coming from my sins, the prayers of others, or from my fore-parents. Lord, sever and destroy every evil thing with all their effect, side effects, stings, roots and tentacles. Lord, burn them at their roots so they cannot come back on my family or me again, in the name of Jesus and through the power of the Holy Spirit. Amen!

Chapter Challenge:

CHAPTER 6: DESTROYING STRONGHOLDS

1) Define the term, "stronghold." How have ungodly strongholds influenced your relationship with God? How have ungodly strongholds influenced your life?

---

2) What is the first step you must take to destroy a stronghold?

---

3) Where do your strongholds hide?

_____

_____

_____

_____

_____

_____

_____

_____

_____

4) What was Elijah's consequence of allowing strongholds to manifest in his life? Do you want the same fate?

_____

_____

_____

_____

_____

_____

_____

_____

_____

5) What steps did the author provide that would destroy strongholds in your life?

_____

_____

_____

_____

_____

_____

_____

_____

_____

Prayer Starter: Lord Jesus, help me to identify the strongholds at work in my life and help me to break their bond on me so that I might live the best life I can and demonstrate your power and healing to all those around me. Help me to have the will and discipline to declare war and fight the good fight against old habits that have been with me as long as I remember. My desire is to live in victory and I know you desire that same goal. I declare victory over strongholds that have hindered me in the past and I break asunder their control over my life. In Jesus' name, I pray. Amen.

Chapter Challenge:

CHAPTER 7: RELEASE THE BLOOD OF JESUS

1) What are Satan's strongest weapons toward you?

_____

_____

_____

_____

_____

_____

_____

_____

_____

2) How have you been made perfect before God?

_____

_____

_____

_____

_____

_____

_____

_____

_____

3) Why Is Satan called the accuser of the brethren? What accusations has he whispered to you?

_____

_____

_____

_____

_____

_____

_____

_____

_____

4) By releasing the blood of Jesus, what happens to Satan? Why is the blood of Jesus an effective tool in breaking generational curses?

_____

_____

_____

_____

_____

_____

_____

_____

_____

5) Have you ever been the victim of condemnation and/or guilt? How has the victim role hindered your progress of fulfilling your destiny?

_____

_____

_____

_____

_____

_____

_____

_____

_____

Prayer Starter: Heavenly Father, I thank you for the forgiveness that was purchased for me on Calvary through the blood of your son Jesus Christ. I thank you that today and forever I stand before you holy and forgiven—cleansed from all sin and guilt. I declare your blood over my life now and ask you to help me remember that I am, and always will be, your child. You have promised never to leave me nor forsake me, so I am secure in my eternal relationship with you. When I struggle against my flesh, help to always remember who I am—that your son's blood covers me forever. Thank you for salvation. Thank you for being my father. Thank you for forgiveness and that my salvation is not dependent on my strength but on your mighty strength. In Jesus' name. Amen.

Chapter Challenge:

CHAPTER 8: SPEAKING GOD'S TRUTH ABOUT YOU TO YOURSELF

1) What do you gain from asking yourself empowering questions daily?

_____

_____

_____

_____

_____

_____

_____

_____

_____

2) What is the only offensive weapon in the Christian arsenal?

_____

_____

_____

_____

_____

_____

_____

_____

_____

3) How can you use God's word to transform your life? Which scriptures do you need to speak over yourself daily?

_____

_____

_____

_____

_____

_____

_____

_____

_____

4) When you speak negative, cruel joking or destructive words to children, how does that impact their lives? Are you the victim of someone speaking those words over you?

_____

_____

_____

_____

_____

_____

_____

_____

_____

5) What does it mean to renew your mind? List five positive advantages you will have when you renew your mind.

_____

_____

_____

_____

_____

_____

_____

_____

_____

_____

Prayer Starter: Father God in the name of Jesus, I ask you Lord to please forgive me in any way that I was not a good steward over my mouth or my words. Lord, I pray that you would set a guard over my mouth and watch the doors of my lips so that I won't stumble in thought, word or deed. Give me a willing spirit that is hungry and thirsty for the word of God. Help me to speak what is pleasing to you, no matter what the circumstance is. Thank you for teaching me how to guard my mouth. In Jesus' name, Amen.

Chapter Challenge:

CHAPTER 9: OBEDIENCE – THE ACCESS TO YOUR SUCCESS

1) Why is it important to obey God?

_____

_____

_____

_____

_____

_____

_____

_____

_____

2) List three blessings associated with obedience. List three curses associated with disobedience.

_____

_____

_____

_____

_____

_____

_____

_____

_____

3) What is the secret to pleasing God? Provide a scriptural reference.

_____

_____

_____

_____

_____

_____

_____

_____

_____

4) How do you know if you love God with all of your heart, soul and mind?

_____

_____

_____

_____

_____

_____

_____

_____

_____

5) What would happen to your life if you treated others the way you want to be treated? What benefits would you reap?

_____

_____

_____

_____

_____

_____

_____

_____

_____

Prayer Starter: Father God, in the name of Jesus, I thank you God for giving me another opportunity to make it right with you. Father, I ask that you would help me to love my neighbors and love myself. Help me to be kind, gentle, do justice, love mercy and to walk humbly with you all of the days of my life. Thank you for liberating me from psychological, mental and emotional prisons that have kept me in bondage for so long. It is now that I walk in my freedom. In Jesus' name, Amen.

Chapter Challenge:

CHAPTER 10

1) As the first step in the process, what must you identify to overcome life's issues?

_____

_____

_____

_____

_____

_____

_____

_____

_____

2) How can you break the cycle of generational dysfunction and curses?

_____

_____

_____

_____

_____

_____

_____

_____

_____

3) Are you synchronizing your faith to God's Word? Or, are you finding your fulfillment in "stuff?" List five things God wants to share with you?

_____

_____

_____

_____

_____

_____

_____

4) How can you gain confidence and reassurance to win the victory? What four things must you do?

_____

_____

_____

_____

_____

_____

_____

_____

_____

5) Have you practiced recently to overcome the RESISTANCE that seeks to destroy your life? If so, what has opened up for you?

_____

_____

_____

_____

_____

_____

_____

_____

_____